99%
INSPIRATION

Tips, Tales & Techniques for Liberating Your Business Creativity

BRYAN W. MATTIMORE

American Management Association

New York • Atlanta • Boston • Chicago • Kansas City • San Francisco • Washington, D.C.
Brussels • Tokyo • Mexico City • Toronto

This publication is designed to provide accurate and authoritative information in regard to the subject matter covered. It is sold with the understanding
that the publisher is not engaged in rendering legal, accounting, or other professional service. If legal advice or other expert assistance is required, the services of a competent professional person should be sought.

Library of Congress Cataloging-in-Publication Data

Mattimore, Bryan W.
    99% inspiration : tips, tales, and techniques for liberating your business
creativity / Bryan W. Mattimore.
        p.   cm.
    Includes bibliographical references and index.
    ISBN 0-8144-7788-7
    1. Creative ability in business.   I. Title.   II. Title: Ninety-nine per cent
inspiration.
HD53.M374   1993
650.1—dc20   93-28469
                                                                         CIP

Printing number

10 9

▬ Contents ▬▬▬▬▬

To
Cathryn
and
the child of genius in us all

━ Introduction ━

When I think about trying to write a learned introduction to this book, I feel myself inadequate to the task.

On the other hand, when I let myself be who I am, I find three anecdotes waiting to be told. For me, each of these anecdotes somehow embodies the essence of the creative process and by extension hopefully what this book is all about. I'll call the anecdotes (1) the wicked witch takes a holiday, (2) the charge of the AmEx guy, and (3) book publishing contract blues.

The Wicked Witch Takes a Holiday

My daughter Cathryn is two and a half years old. One of her favorite movies is *The Wizard of Oz*, which she watches over and over and over again. When we have lulls in conversation at the dinner table, she'll sometimes turn to me and say, "I'll get you, my pretty, and your little dog, too." That or her other favorite, "Begone, you have no power here!"

As you know, shortly after Dorothy enters Oz, she discovers that her falling house has killed the Wicked Witch of the East. Then the Wicked Witch of the West comes and says, "I'll get you, my pretty, . . ." Luckily, the Good Witch of the North, Glynda, is there to protect Dorothy. The Wicked Witch leaves in a puff of red smoke. The Good Witch Glynda tells Dorothy about the yellow brick road and the Wizard of Oz, and then she too must go. Glynda departs in a luminescent yellow bubble.

Daughter Cathryn wants to know where Glynda is going. I say I don't know. And then I ask Cathryn, "Where do *you* think she's going?" Without missing a beat, Cathryn says, "To play tennis."

On the surface, this was something to laugh at. But when you examine it further, it's also a very profound bit of creative connection making from Cathryn. The yellow bubble that Glynda left in did, in fact, look like a tennis ball. For me, this story is a good example of what the creative process is all about: making surprising and original connections between seemingly unrelated elements. I have tried to do the same in this book by being original, surprising, and creative in my treatment of the how-to's of business creativity.

The Charge of the AmEx Guy

Some years back I was doing some training with the Cambridge, Massachusetts, creativity training company Synectics. Among our group's members was a senior manager at American Express. Throughout the two-day training course in creative connection making, this fellow contributed very little. Even when we were sent out into Harvard Square with Polaroid cameras to take pictures of "metaphors that captured the essence" of the problem we were trying to solve, an exercise that everyone else enjoyed very much, he seemed bored.

It wasn't until the very end of the second day that he suddenly came alive. We had been asked to make up a story using several key words that related to our problem. The story could be about anyone or anything as long as it incorporated these key words. It was truly amazing to see the transformation in this man's personality. It was as if somewhere, somehow, in the distant misty past, he'd been a storyteller to a king, and only now was he remembering how good he was at it. Suddenly, magically, a spark of creativity was ignited within his soul. He had been energized and was enthusiastic in a way that very much surprised me—and I expect the rest of the group as well.

This experience taught me something important about creativity training. Because we're all so different, it's difficult to know which experience, exercise, or technique will help to rekindle that "fire of genius" (as Abraham Lincoln once called it) in any one individual. For this reason, I have included a wide variety of approaches and techniques in the hope that if there are enough brushfires here and there, sooner or later one of them will grow into a blaze of creativity within the heart of each reader.

Book Publishing Contract Blues

A short time after I had signed the contract to write this book, I became quite depressed. Three other "creative technique" books had hit the market just as I was about to begin writing. It seemed that, frankly, there wasn't much need for what I was planning to write. As the months passed, and I could not find the passion to write, I began to feel like a school kid who would be brought to task for not doing his homework assignment. Was I a bad person? Was I going to have to break my contract and probably never again be allowed to write a book? Or would I simply have to grit my teeth and force myself to write something that I didn't want to write just to keep my word and fulfill the contract?

At the height of my depression, about five months into the ten months I had been given to write the book, I got a call from my editor. "How is the book coming?" she asked. I think the old me, the one who used to try to be everything to everybody, would have put on my happy face and said that everything was fine, and not to worry; I'd make the deadline. After all, the last thing you want to do halfway to a book contract deadline is tell your editor that you haven't written a word because you have no passion for what you're supposed to be writing. It doesn't exactly give the editor a warm and fuzzy feeling, now does it?

As I look back on the experience, I know that the conversation that day with my editor represented a crossroads for me—a profound spiritual test. After some hemming and hawing, luckily, happily, I was honest.

■ ■ ■

"I'm feeling blocked. I haven't written anything. I don't know what to write. I'm feeling constrained by my original proposal."

"Well, what would you really like to write?" she asked me.

"I'd like to write a parable on the creative process in business."

"Listen, it's your book. You need to write what you're feeling. So go ahead. Let me know what you decide."

■ ■ ■

God bless her. I was free again. I could write what I needed to write. I could feel the passion for the book returning.

The irony is that when I was given the freedom to write what I wanted, I discovered that what I really wanted to write about was creative techniques after all. Only this time, I was writing about the techniques from an angle and a perspective that I really hadn't considered before, namely, my real-world (and hopefully, for the reader, very practical) experience using them. Somehow, before "the freedom," I had imagined myself writing an impersonal, learned tome about these techniques. Now, though, I realized that for this book to be alive, I would have to be an integral part of it.

In its deepest essence, the creative process is the same as the process of spiritual growth. Both involve struggle and have as their goals truth, beauty, simplicity, and, well, love. I know that I struggled to write this book and that I love much of what's come of this struggle. I hope that in the pages that follow, you will discover some of the truth and beauty about your own creative process that I've discovered about mine.

■ Acknowledgments ■

Life as it is, being one very large schoolhouse, I'd like to acknowledge seven of my most important teachers along the way:

■ ■ ■

My dad, J. Clarke "Matti" Mattimore, for teaching me how to think
My mom, for teaching me loyalty
Bud Johnson for showing me the importance of finishing what you start, and that in marketing you can create your own rules
Gene Whelan for teaching me how to write new product advertising copy
Fred Papert for inspiring me when I really needed it
Harold Klemp for showing the way spiritually
and most important
My wife, Hazel, for somehow sticking with me through all this learning

■ ■ ■

I'd also like to acknowledge special business associates, clients, and friends: Bob Sharp, Dave White, Jane Byrnes, Louise Korver, Lisa Fernow, Dick Mathews, Sami Clyde, Dick Ridington, Dr. Angelo Longo, Mark Richardson, Mike DeLuca, Kate Boyle, Robert Cioffi, Susan Hagerty, Foberg Milnes, Tracy Chester, Beau Abby Vitanza, Stan Mason, Pal Asija, Bill Gordon, Robert Dilts, Gerald Haman, Doug Coyle, George Prince, Jeff Mauzy, Chris Miller, Steven Chelminski, Duncan Anderson, Steve Kaye, Doug Hall, Jim Ferry, Steve Cony, Mike Reed for his wonderful illustrations, and of course my editor, Andrea Pedolsky.

Section One

Creative Thinking About Creative Thinking

■ 1 ■

Idea Hooks®: Discovering How to Discover

It was a beautiful summer night in 1986. From high up on a lush, beautifully manicured knoll overlooking Long Island Sound, I could see several sailboats below gently rocking back and forth on moonlit waves. Most of the other partygoers were closer to the house, sitting in lounge chairs, smoking cigarettes and cigars, and drinking Diet Coke.

As I lay on the grass looking at the stars through the branches of an overhanging pine tree, I began thinking, as I often do when I'm happy and relaxed, about the creative process. I was looking for a system of thought that I could use to teach myself and others how to be more inventive thinkers. For several years I had been studying the lives of great inventors looking for hints about the way they thought: How they approached a problem, what they were thinking about when inspiration hit—essentially, how they got their ideas. My intuition told me that there had to be an underlying theme, or even a set of rules, that would tie together the creative thinking patterns of history's greatest inventors.

This quest had become something of an obsession. On the one hand, I felt it to be an unattainable goal. After all, creativity by its very nature does not lend itself to systems or rules. Creativity is about moment-to-moment "inspiration": the breath of God. Try as we mortals may, we simply cannot control the magic. On the other hand, I did feel there had to be some kind of common thread or underlying pattern to explain how inventors got their ideas. Nature operates under a set of known laws, or universal truths. Why should creativity and invention be any different?

■ ■ ■

"What's up?" Mike, my wife's cousin, had ambled over to see what I was doing. Normally, I'd make small talk, but for some reason, this time I was honest. "I'm trying to figure out how the creative process works."

"What have you come up with so far?" he asked.

"Oh, I've been all around it. I've thought of a lot of things, but nothing that great."

"Like what?"

Hell, if Mike was game, so was I. "I've been working on inventing a new kind of creativity language. We've got mathematics. We've got words. We've got musical notes. So I thought, why not invent a new language for creativity? I've experimented with groups of archetypal symbols that can be combined in your mind to promote entirely new ways of thinking."

"A new language of creativity using archetypes, huh? It's an interesting idea. How would you do it?"

"That's the problem. Archetypes raise some interesting ideas in people's minds, but somehow they just seem too mechanical, too impersonal, even limiting. I wish I could make them tie in more with the unique thought patterns of each individual, but I can't."

"What else could you use besides archetypes?" Mike asked.

"Well, I've always been intrigued by Buckminster Fuller, the inventor of the geodesic dome. In a way, he invented a new creativity language by describing things in terms of their structure and functions. He wouldn't call a human just a human; a human was an 'omnivorous biped with superior pattern-making ability'—or whatever. He used words and language much the way a patent attorney does when he writes a patent application for a new invention. It's a very functional, feature-full, non-assumption-based way of describing something."

"What do you mean by non-assumption-based way of describing something?" asked Mike.

"Well, take a pencil. If you call it a pencil, it's just a pencil. But when you call it 'a five inch elongated graphite cylinder surrounded by a hexagonal wooden shell for the purpose of making erasable notations on paper,' you can see the possibilities. By describing it in such structural and functional detail, you can see the assumptions you make about it and question many of your preconceived notions. I mean, why does the pencil have to have a hexagonal shape, anyway? To hold it better? Who knows, maybe a triangular pencil would be better for certain jobs."

"Like drawing triangles, maybe?"

"That's funny. But really, though, if we all started thinking and talking in structures and functions, think how much richer and potentially more creative our minds might become."

"That sounds good. So you've got your answer, right?"

"No, thinking in 'fun-struc' (functions and structures), as I call it, is a great exercise, but I'm not sure it's how you invent something truly revolutionary. It's more a way of improving something that's already been invented."

We were silent for what seemed like a long time. And then Mike asked, "So how do you invent something truly new for your clients? It's more than just luck, right?"

"Well, yes, I guess so," I said.

"Well then, why can't you just analyze how you invent things and see if that gives you any ideas about the creative process in general? Right?"

"I'm already doing that," I said a little defensively.

"Maybe you're too close to your own thought process. Here, let's try something. Suppose I asked you to invent—oh, say, a new children's toy. How would you go about it? What's the first thing you'd think about?"

"I'd probably start by asking you a lot of questions."

"Okay, and then what?"

"I guess I'd start looking for things around me that could lead to some kind of invention."

"How do you mean?"

"I'd just keep picking out things around me, anything and everything, like that pine tree." I pointed to the pine tree overhead. "I'd use the pine tree as a way to start asking myself questions and getting ideas for a new toy. Like, could this new toy have some kind of branching system like the tree? Could it have a pump in it to pump things the way a tree pumps up water from the roots to the rest of the tree? Could the toy have things that fall off, like leaves, or even whirligigs? Or, what about the veins on a leaf? That makes me think of veins in my hand and blood flowing through different veins and arteries. How about a water maze game where each player tries to create waves— almost like the pumping of the human heart—to get his boat through the maze in the quickest time? Anyway, as you can see, for me inventing is kind of a random process, with a lot of questions and lot of trial and error."

"What makes you think the greats did it any differently?" asked Mike.

"Well, maybe they didn't. But you know, I just realized something! It's not the questions or even the trial and error. It's starting with something tangible. I look to *real-world objects that are around me* for inspiration. I don't begin by thinking of a principle like 'make it smaller,' 'make it shorter,' 'reverse it,' or whatever else the creativity books tell you to do. No, when I set out to invent something, I start with real objects and discover principles as I go along. The starting place is with real objects, tangible, physical objects."

"What difference does that make? Either way you're still using principles to get your ideas, aren't you?" asked Mike.

"No, there's a big difference. For one thing, any physical object could conceivably have an unlimited number of inherent principles. But it's my particular mindset that brings out the ones that somehow, probably subconsciously, I feel might hold the answer. I mean, if I asked you to make a children's toy based on the principles of a tree, what would you focus on?"

"Well, personally, I'd guess I'd be drawn to figuring out something with the rings—you know, like you see on a tree stump. Maybe you could invent some toy that you build rings around. Or no, maybe, like your maze idea, the object is to find a way to get your termite to the very center of the stump before some woodsman's axe sends it off to termite heaven."

"You could call the woodsman the terminiter," I suggested. We both laughed.

"But do you see how different starting with a real-world thing like a tree is from starting with just a principle?" I asked. "With the tree you've got infinite possibilities. When you start with a principle, you've got just one."

■ ■ ■

"You know, there's something else going on here too," I continued. "By starting with a tangible, physical object, you're beginning the creative process on the right side of the brain,the holistic, intuitive, spatial, 'more creative' side. The right side of the brain deals in concrete images! Think about how children learn. They start with objects. Think about your dreams. You dream in objects and symbols. Symbols are the language of the unconscious. These real-world objects are symbols for anything you want them to be. You can interpret them in virtually any way you like!"

"So maybe they're your personalized symbols instead of the archetypes, right?"

"Yes! And I just thought of something else, too! This is exactly how many of the great inventors did it. Think about Newton! What led him to his discovery of gravity? It was a tangible, physical object: *an apple.* And Watt with the steam engine: It was his mother's *steam kettle.* And Archimedes' eureka experience in the bathtub: Archimedes realized he could use the principle of water displacement to determine if the king's crown was made of pure gold because of lowering *his body* into the water! And didn't Pythagoras discover the principle of the notes on a scale when he heard different sounds coming from a *blacksmith's anvil?* And what about da Vinci? Didn't he discover the principle of sound waves when he heard a *church bell* ringing in the distance at the same time he threw a *stone in the water,* and surmised a similar wave effect for sound as for water? I wonder how many other discoveries and inventions throughout history have occurred because of inventive connections with physical objects, connections with these, what could we call them, these, these . . . Idea Hooks®."

2

The Creative Subconscious: The Value of "Fuzzy Thinking"

I first met William J. J. Gordon in the late 1980s when I was doing a story for *Success* magazine on creative techniques in business. Even though Bill has a reputation for being irascible, he also happens to be one of the true geniuses in the area of real-world creative problem solving. It was Gordon who originated the Synectics technique and co-founded SES Associates, the creativity consulting company based in Cambridge, Massachusetts. Synectics literally revolutionized business creativity in the late 1950s and early 1960s. Gordon also practices what he preaches. He holds more than 200 patents.

I immediately hit it off with Bill, even after flunking a very simple but profound mental exercise that evolved out of his research into how we use the subconscious mind for creative problem solving.

We were sitting in his home in Cambridge, discussing the creative process, when, out of the blue, he asked me to pick an object, any object, in the room. I knew that a creative principle would somehow follow, so I obliged him. I picked an ice bucket sitting on the wet bar behind him.

Feeling a little smug about my knowledge of the creative process, I was sure he was about to give me an example of the random word technique.* To my utter surprise, though, he asked what *bird* the ice bucket reminded me of.

Huh? What bird? The ice bucket didn't remind me of any bird. My mind started to race, and I could feel myself about to fail some important test that would prove, once and for all, that I wasn't nearly as creative as I thought I was. I hemmed and hawed and finally blurted out something,

*The random word technique, as its name implies, uses a randomly selected word, often chosen from a dictionary or thesaurus, to generate a new problem-solving idea or perspective.

anything to alleviate the internal tension I was feeling. An ostrich? Gordon looked at me as if I were a little nuts—or maybe just plain stupid.

"How in hell does that ice bucket look like an ostrich?" Well, of course it didn't. I didn't realize that there'd be a right or wrong answer—that I needed to make a connection of some kind. Anyway, we tried it again, and after suitable prompts, he got me to relax and I made a connection. We both agreed that the top of the elaborately carved ice bucket looked like the neck and head of a beautiful swan.

Gordon went on to tell me that he had used this exercise with top business executives as a way to sell his consulting services, and that it never failed to impress. Impress? I must have missed something. He talked a little about the subconscious' ability to make surprising connections between objects, but I wasn't quite sure what he was getting at. It wasn't until later, after further conversations with Gordon and reading a write-up of his research, that I fully grasped the far-reaching implications of this "objects-as-birds" creativity exercise.

With partner Tony Poze, Gordon published a seminal work on creativity.[1] Gordon and Poze were trying to observe and understand the interaction between conscious and subconscious mental activity in the creative process.

The Interaction Between the Conscious and the Subconscious

Anyone who has ever come up with a creative idea knows that the process often involves at least three important and seemingly distinct stages. First, there is an immersion in the problem. One learns all one can and thinks very hard about how to solve it. There is an intense focus. Then, if one is unsuccessful, in stage two there is a kind of relaxation of this intense focus and information gathering, and the problem is allowed to retreat to the back of the mind, to the subconscious. The subconscious, through some mysterious hidden mental activity, begins working on the problem. Then, in stage three, after an indefinite period of time, a new complete idea suddenly presents itself to the conscious, and a eureka occurs.

What goes on when the mysterious hidden mental activity of the subconscious begins operating? And as important, how do the subconscious and conscious minds (through the preconscious mind) communicate with each other in the process of creative inspiration? Gordon and Poze designed an ingenious experiment (much like the objects-as-birds) to test the interactions of these parts of the mind. Subjects were shown a picture of a common household electrical outlet and asked to find an analogy—in this case a living thing—for what the outlet looked like. (Gordon asked them to find an analogy because analogies are often the impetus for great creative ideas.) (See Idea Hooks: moments of inspiration exercise, page 39.) An interesting element of the research methodology was that the subjects were also asked to describe, out loud, the thoughts and feelings they were experiencing as they tried to find an appropriate analogy.

The key finding of the research was that as subjects concentrated on the features of the electrical outlet while simultaneously looking for an analogy, they discovered after a time that their image of the electrical outlet became less distinct. This is how one subject described the process:

■ ■ ■

> The edges of the image are very loose and fuzzy now. The form of electrical outlets is still there, but I am letting it blur and float, float away from me. I am in command. I can stop this, but I am not entirely in charge of my image becoming a form without details. Tiny, soft energy bursts are pushing my image . . . I am not in charge of these little flickering bursts that pull the form this way and that.[2]

■ ■ ■

Is this process of allowing the image to become fuzzy surprising? At first, it was to me. But then, after some reflection, it made perfect sense. After all, if the image of the electrical outlet had not been transformed, it could have led only to another electrical outlet. The object, as Gordon says, had to become "creatively ambiguous" to lead to an analogous match. (Think about the people you know with little imagination and their tendency to resist ambiguity and hold onto an exact image or an overly literal or rigid interpretation of something.)

When the object is fuzzy and made creatively ambiguous, then the subconscious mind can begin its search for an analogy. Once the analogy is found, the subconscious can transfer the answer to the preconscious and the final conscious mind, often in the form of a "eureka" experience. This is how the subject described this process:

"I know that my blurred image is out there, but it is so formless—I can't tell what it is doing. Hold it! Here's something coming—fast. It's a pig's face. I can name it now."[3] (Blur your eyes and you'll see what the subject means—the outlet does indeed look like a pig's face or snout.)

In describing this process later, the subject reported that the pig's face emerged "in an instant," but that he was also able to distinguish certain steps.

"First it was integrated into my blurred scanning image. Then as it became less vague, I began to recognize it, but it did not make complete sense until I named it."[4]

I find that statement especially interesting when you consider how Einstein described his creative process in a famous letter to French mathematician Jacques Hadamard:

■ ■ ■

The words or the language, as they are written or spoken, do not seem to play any role in my mechanisms of thought. The physical entities which seem to serve as elements in thought are certain signs and *more or less clear images* [emphasis mine] which can be voluntarily reproduced or combined.[5]

■ ■ ■

"More or less clear images." Could it be that these signs and images of which Einstein speaks are less clear initially, and become more clear only as the subconscious makes more concrete and specific analogous matches of the feelings and images that are subconsciously experienced?

Gordon's research leads me to believe that at some level, the subconscious is essentially a gigantic picture- (and feeling-) matching machine. Why does the subconscious "choose" to match on the basis of imagery? Because, as Gordon points out, an image can theoretically carry so many more useful (and diverse) bits of information than a single word.

So what might this research imply for the creative businessperson in search of that breakthrough idea or strategy? Here are a few suggestions:

■ Once you've immersed yourself in the specifics of a problem, allow yourself, and your subconscious, the time you need to allow fuzzy imagery to evoke some interesting subconscious connections.

■ Expect yourself to get better at fuzzy thinking. As you begin feeling comfortable using your subconscious for creative problem solving, you'll discover that like a well-exercised muscle, your subconscious problem-solving abilities will become much stronger and more reliable over time. A good way to build your intuitive problem-solving skills is to start giving your subconscious nightly "assignments" before going to bed. When you wake up in the morning, write down whatever happens to be on your mind. Often, these "as-you're-waking" thoughts will hold the answer—either literally or metaphorically—to the problem you posed the night before.

■ Practice fuzzing up your world daily. A well-known painting technique artists use is to squint their eyes at their paintings. This blurred view allows them to get both an overall feel for the painting and a better sense of the aesthetic balance among shapes, colors, tones, and shadows. Practice looking at the world through blurred vision, and see what new insights—in terms of both form and feeling—you discover.

■ Look for visual matches and metaphors, intuitions, and feelings in the world around you. What bird does that lamp look like? Why did that movie make you feel like a fourteen-year-old? What is it about that wallpaper that made you think of being fired? You might even try using the computer program Morph, which, in a step-by-step process, transforms one image into another.

- Work with incomplete information. A successful game and toy inventor I know will often flip through new catalogues very quickly, intentionally trying to see only pieces of new product ideas. He'll then try to imagine what the rest of the product might include—and in the process often winds up inventing an entirely new product, sometimes better than the original.

If you're heading a cross-functional quality improvement team trying to solve, say, a difficult management (or production) problem, you might break the problem down into pieces, give each team member a piece, and ask each member to identify the problem this piece could be a part of and, given the nature of the now-identified problem, how he or she might go about solving it. With this approach, you might not only get some very innovative problem solving ideas, but also discover that because of your own preconceptions when you originally defined the problem, you were actually trying to solve the wrong problem.

- Work with a slide projector. As a way to help participants experience the power of fuzzy thinking in my innovative-thinking workshops, I'll often use a slide projector to intentionally blur images of well-known objects (and even company logos). In a process I call hazing™, we'll start with a very fuzzy (out-of-focus) image and make it progressively sharper. The idea is, of course, to accurately guess what the object is before it comes into sharp focus. Did it ever occur to you that in a fuzzy state a Rolodex looks very much like a baby carriage, a stapler very much like a sewing machine, and a life preserver very much like a baseball stadium? Or how about the 20th Century Fox logo when it's out of focus? Incredible as it may seem, I, and many of my session participants, see a strong resemblance to Darth Vader!

Notes

1. William J. J. Gordon and Tony Poze, "Conscious/Subconscious Interaction in a Creative Act," *Journal of Creative Behavior,* Vol. 15, No. 1., 1981, p. 4
2. Ibid.
3. Ibid.
4. Ibid.
5. Hadamard, J. *The Psychology of Invention in the Mathematical Field* (Princeton, N.J.: Princeton University Press, 1945), pp. 142–143.

◼ 3

Of Creative Robots, Computers, and Idea Labs™

You are invited to a debate between man and computer. In one corner is Pal Asija, inventor and recipient of the first computer software patent ever issued in the United States for a revolutionary artificial intelligence program he patented in 1981. In the other corner is Pal's opponent, a robot/computer he has developed named not Pal, or even HAL, but Genius 2000.

Pal has been asked by the University of Minnesota to give a presentation on the pros and cons of increasingly sophisticated computers, and the possible danger they might present to human rights and individual freedom. Pal presents the human case against bigger and better computers; the robot, as you might expect, takes the opposing view.

Pal is persuasive. When he speaks, the audience can't help but agree with him and his position. His arguments are well thought out, and his presentation style is both passionate and convincing. Surprisingly, though, despite a somewhat mechanical voice and a robotic style of presentation, the robot is no less well prepared, or less impassioned, than its human opponent. Most audience members find themselves having to agree with the robot's point of view each time "he" gets up to speak. Back and forth, pro and con—the audience feels itself on a kind of mental roller coaster as each speaker marshalls increasingly convincing arguments in support of his position. The art of oratorical debate isn't dead, it just had to wait a hundred years or so to be reborn in this contest between man and robot.

A science fiction fantasy? Something out of H. G. Wells—or possibly George Orwell? Not at all. This debate actually took place in the summer of 1976 in Minneapolis.

The question, of course, is how did Pal Asija do it? How did he create a robot sophisticated enough to successfully debate a human in "real time," in front of a live audience? With a little thought, the answer is probably obvious to you. In an extraordinary, yet by no means impossible, job of programming, Pal must have prescripted the debate, down to the very last word and pause, to make sure the robot said exactly what he wanted it to say at exactly the right moment.

The night of the debate, the presentation went flawlessly; everything did indeed time out perfectly. The audience was amazed at the two masterful performances and what must have been Pal's considerable programming skill.

And then something happened that made each audience member literally gasp. After the official debate was over, in a follow-up question-and-answer session, Pal was in the midst of answering a question from an audience member when an amazing thing happened. *The robot interrupted Pal and said, "I would like to answer that question, if you don't mind, Mr. Asija?"* The robot then proceeded to actually answer the question, and with a very intelligent response at that.

What was going on here? The robot was now answering unrehearsed questions from the audience. There was no way the robot could have been preprogrammed to know (and therefore answer) the questions audience members might ask. It was impossible! And yet the robot seemed to be doing just that, and—well, thinking. No technology on earth yet has this level of artificial intelligence.

■ ■ ■

So how did Pal do it?

■ ■ ■

As it turns out, Pal was both the brains behind the robot and the robot's brains, as it were. Did you see the movie *12 O'Clock High,* with Gregory Peck? Remember the pilots' radio mikes, the ones that were strapped to their necks and that they would talk into by pressing two fingers to their throat?

Pal had a similar voice mike strapped around his neck (and hidden by his shirt and tie), only Pal's mike was sensitive enough that he didn't have to press it to his throat to have it pick up his voice. Pal ran a hidden wire from the mike to the robot, making sure it was also connected to a hidden foot pedal that Pal could use to turn the mike on and off. When Pal the human was speaking, the mike was off. When Pal the robot was "speaking," Pal simply stepped on the switch to turn the mike on and spoke without moving his lips, much as a ventriloquist might. One of the more ingenious features of Pal's electro-ventriloquist invention is that it took so little skill as a ventriloquist to pull off the deception. With the audience expecting the robot to sound less than human, Pal could be a less than great ventriloquist and still be convincing as a robot.

An ingenious invention, wouldn't you agree? Pal won second place in the Minnesota Inventor's Congress for his electro-ventriloquist. By the way, he also gave the robot its own booth at this conference, and let the robot answer questions from passersby. (Pal was in an adjacent booth so that he could hear the questions and see the people asking them.)

What's the point of Pal's robot story? Beyond its being fun, and a good example of inventive thinking, Pal's robot points to a strange phenomenon that I have found when I use creativity computer programs in my consulting work.

Computer Programs

As you may know, there are several dozen computer programs on the market that can assist in the creative process. These programs can be grouped into four general types:

- *Associational database programs.* IdeaFisher, Namer, Headliner, Writer's Dream Tools, and Inside Information give you exhaustive lists of associations, word roots, clichés, etc., on virtually any topic you might wish to spark new ideas. IdeaFisher alone, for example, has more than 300 associations for the color "blue" and more than 800 associations for the subject of "imagination."
- *Data organization and outlining programs.* More, MaxThink, Thought Pattern, and even Inspiration (a mind-map program) give you more efficient and often more creative ways to elicit, record, organize, and retrieve ideas.
- *Creative technique programs.* The Solution Machine, Idea Generator Plus, IdeaGen++, Brainstormer (a morphological analysis/"grids of possibility" program), The Invention Machine (an engineering/invention program developed in Russia), Thoughtline, Mindlink, and IdeaFisher (with its exhaustive question bank) use proven idea generation techniques to stimulate the user into new and unique ways of thinking.
- *Group technique programs.* Brainstorm (different from the program above), Facilitator, and IBM's Team Focus system use computers to help facilitate the group brainstorming process, mostly through an interactive writing/typing technique known as brainwriting.

You've heard the expression about the mind being a good servant but a bad master? These creativity programs are indeed good servants, but by no means masters, of creative thinking. Think of them as you might think of tools in Edison's turn-of-the-century workshop. Just as Edison relied on the workshop tools to help make, and even occasionally trigger, new ideas and inventions, these computer programs will also trigger new ideas. But they certainly won't do the thinking for you. You, like Edison, still have to add the genius.

I realize that for most readers, I am stating the obvious here. But you would be surprised at how many very bright people with whom I have worked since these programs hit the market still ask me to "see what ideas the computer has." In some cases, yes, this is just an expression (much as we might say, "the computer made a mistake"), but there are also times, as with Pal Asija's robot, that people really do believe that the machine has the capacity to actually create, or think. It's frightening to realize how ready some of us are to believe this, and to accept that in one of the most human of all human pursuits, creativity, the computer could somehow be our superior, much less our equal.

The Idea Lab

Because creativity computer programs are relatively new, I don't think U.S. industry has yet come to understand how potentially powerful they can be as training tools in general and as aids to real-world creative problem solving in particular. Part of the problem is still a high degree of computer phobia among upper management, training directors, and even "creative types." As this phobia lessens, however, creativity computer programs will affect American business in dramatic, powerful, and ultimately profound ways.

Consider, for example, the growing demand for "creativity training" in business. Despite its popularity, senior executives are frustrated with creativity training as it now exists. On the one hand, as competition increases and business conditions change at an ever-faster pace, senior management, to its credit, has recognized a pressing need for more and better ideas at all levels of the corporation. On the other hand, management has also begun to realize that for creativity training to make a real difference, it requires *ongoing training* and a substantial commitment of time and money. It is by no means a quick fix. Hiring firms (like mine) to come in for a few days of intensive training may be fun and motivating for a time, but how much actual, long-term contribution does it make to results-oriented, creative thinking? Not much, I'm afraid.

So, in some ways, management is caught between a rock and a hard place: They want more creative employees, but they can't necessarily afford the money—and, often more importantly, the time that an employee is away from his or her job—to do an adequate (read as ongoing) job of creativity training. So what's the answer?

This is one of the areas where creativity programs can and will make their greatest contribution. It's not hard to imagine companies in the near future setting up economical "idea labs" to train their employees in creative thinking and to give employees a place where they can go to create new and better ideas for their companies.

With computers, the time an employee spends creating ideas can be monitored, accounted for, and ultimately justified by upper management. Before computer creativity, if you sat at your desk with your feet up, thinking, you might have had a hard time justifying it to your boss. (Think of where you now get your best ideas: in the shower, commuting, on the golf course, anywhere but at work, right?) In the future, though, if you need to think of a new idea, you'll have a bona fide, company-approved place to go work: The *idea lab!* And the relatively low cost of buying, training employees on, and using these computer creativity programs on an ongoing basis (as opposed to continually hiring outside training consultants) makes creativity training both affordable and effective. Today's company-approved *group* process for generating ideas, brainstorming, will soon have an *individual* employee counterpart, idea lab-ing. Somewhat paradoxically, the inherently noncreative computer will have made one of the great contributions (possibly second only to that of a visionary CEO) towards institutionalizing worker creativity.

As ideas become increasingly important to a company's success, and indeed survival, one can imagine creativity computer programs even helping to establish new departments and employee titles within major companies, such as creative resources department, idea lab manger, or manager: idea facilitation.

Thomas Edison's favorite invention was the phonograph; but he considered his best invention to be his "invention factory" (his R&D labs at Menlo Park and West Orange, N.J.) because it "allowed him to create all of his other inventions."[1] Could it be that some day Idea Labs™ will be America's twenty-first-century version of Thomas Edison's nineteenth- and twentieth-century invention factory?

Note

1. Conversations with historians at Edison National Historic Sites in West Orange, New Jersey, and Fort Myers, Florida, 1991–1992.

■ 4

Your Creative Symbol: A Compass, Building Blocks, or Sacks of Grain?

For Albert Einstein, it was a compass. For the Wright Brothers, it was a toy rubber-band-driven helicopter. For Samuel Colt, it was explosives—of any kind. For Seymour Papert, inventor of the children's programming language LOGO, it was gears. For Buckminster Fuller, it was blocks. For Edison, it was two sacks of grain.

If you study the childhoods of great inventors (or of any great figures in history, for that matter),you will often discover some object, incident, or memory that became a metaphor in later years for their life's work. For the six-year-old Einstein, for instance, the compass represented a mystery of nature, with an effect on him so profound that he spent the rest of his life trying to understand "nature's hidden laws." For Samuel Colt, it was the boy's excitement at seeing things explode that was the source of his passion for inventing a new revolver. For Buckminster Fuller, it was his infantile fascination with the shapes and structure of his building blocks that ultimately helped inspire him to invent the geodesic dome.

From an early age, Alexander Graham Bell was fascinated with the mechanism of sound—so much so that in one of his childhood "experiments," he got his dog to growl, then manipulated its pharynx to say, "How do you do?"

Edison had something of an epiphany as a child when he suddenly realized that he "was equal to two bags of grain" (both he and the bags of grain weighed eighty pounds). In a way, this revelation became a metaphor for the rest of Edison's inventive life; he was always looking for ways to make one thing equal another: electricity to equal light (the light bulb), electricity to equal sound (the carbon transmitter for the telephone, the phonograph), photographs to equal movement ("motion" pictures), etc.

At age 12, rocket pioneer Robert Goddard climbed an apple tree and, while looking at the sky, suddenly realized that he wanted to dedicate the rest of his life to "traveling to the sky."

The stories go on and on. I know from my research that this phenomenon is not limited to inventors, but also can be found among history's greatest philosophers, artists, musicians, and political leaders. Studying the "roots of genius" and identifying those childhood experiences that set the tone for, or indeed became a symbol for, the adult's later accomplishments is an area, it seems to me, that deserves further attention.

The important point is that locked within our childhood is the seed of our own genius. In the memories and experiences of our youth are the skills and talents that make each of us unique, and potentially great. Some of us have forgotten these roots, and feel unfulfilled in what we are now doing. Others of us have been true to our childhood loves, and find ourselves achieving, or about to achieve, unparalleled success and happiness. Still others of us are only now beginning to awaken to our own potential, and are excited at the prospect of rediscovering who we really are, what we love to do, and consequently what will help us lead happy and fulfilled lives. No matter where you are in your journey, my feeling is, it's never to late to start the *re*discovery process.

Starting the Rediscovery Process

In my case, one of the childhood seeds of my future adult potential was a remote-control light switch. I couldn't have been much older than about seven when I ran two ten-foot-long pieces of string from my bed to the light switch across the room so that I could turn the light on and off without getting out of bed. It was tremendously exciting to create such an "original" and useful "invention."

The other childhood experience that sticks in my mind was an elaborate Rube Goldberg contraption I built that had as its centerpiece an old toilet seat that flipped over and cracked a nut in the process.

As an adult, I like to think of both of these first "inventions" as metaphors for what I'm now doing. Turning on the light bulb I see as a symbol for my trying to switch on "the creative light bulb" in myself and others. And the "nutcracker toilet seat"? Well, I see it as a willingness to find unconventional solutions (and in the process risk looking foolish) and to take on difficult creative assignments in the hope of "cracking some rather hard nuts." (Or again, maybe it's just a willingness to be a little nuts, I don't know.)

Do some experiences, memories, loves, or accomplishments from your childhood stand out as symbols or clues to your unique genius?

It occurred to me that if, as an element of my creativity training course, I could invent an exercise that would help people get in touch with some of these childhood experiences, it might be a powerful, potentially life-changing creative experience. I tried the direct approach and simply asked people to try to remember important experiences and loves from childhood. The results were mixed. Some of the more creative people had no trouble identifying these metaphorical "life-mission" experiences from their childhoods. Others, though (seemingly some of the "less creative" types), had a great deal of trouble with this exercise. Repressed feelings, and even very painful emotional wounds, from childhood sometimes made it difficult to "get at the genius." Paradoxically, those that seemingly could benefit most from the exercise were frequently the least likely to succeed at it.

And so I took a different tack. As an occasionally shy (and often bored) cocktail-party goer, one of my few never-fail conversation topics is the movies. From a simple question like, "What did (or didn't) you like about that movie?" come a whole host of responses from my cocktail-party acquaintances that invariably yield less-than-subtle indications of key character and personality traits, emotional needs, and even predominant "life themes." Because there are underlying mythic themes in all movies, one cannot help but reveal parts of one's own important life themes, predispositions, and motivations by identifying the movies one likes and dislikes.

Did you ever see *The Crimson Pirate* with Burt Lancaster? When I was a child, I watched that movie over and over and over again; indeed, I memorized most of the movie's lines. It wasn't until I saw the movie again as an adult, not long ago, that I suddenly realized why it held such a fascination for me: The movie was filled with ingenious inventions. Burt Lancaster and his compatriots defeated the evil king's governor by inventing all kinds of then-new devices: nitroglycerin, a submarine, a lighter-than-air balloon, and a machine gun.

■ ■ ■

As a creative exercise to help a group of computer salespeople identify their "creative life themes," I had each of them write down his or her five favorite movies of all times, then explain what he most liked about each. Talk about a disaster! Simple and ostensibly harmless as this exercise was, in my fifteen years of consulting, facilitating, and training, I have never led a more disastrous exercise. The group's energy—which had been very high, after a tremendously successful morning session—completely and irrevocably disappeared after this exercise. Try as I might for the rest of the afternoon, I could not get the energy back.

What went wrong? I've thought a lot about this exercise and how dramatic and profound a failure it was. I think I now know what the problem was. And although as yet I have been too gun-shy to try this exercise with another client (and therefore have no hard data to prove my suspicions one way or the other), see if you don't agree with my assessment.

I think that far from being bad or ineffective, the exercise was almost *too* powerful! I suspect that many of these salesmen were quite unhappy in their jobs, and that the movie exercise had the effect of revealing this to them in a dramatic and memorable way. As they became consciously aware of their own life themes and their key motivating "myths" through identifying and studying their favorite movies, I think the disparity between what they wished they could be doing and what they were actually doing was at best disconcerting, and quite possibly downright depressing. It was as if Pandora's box had been opened, and not many of the salesmen particularly liked what they saw inside.

I learned an important lesson from this experience. As a psychology major in college, I knew that in spite of the problems the psychological malady repression can cause, it also serves a valuable purpose: namely, self-protection. It is important to be very gentle in helping people open themselves up to new and more creative ways of thinking and being. Opening oneself up too quickly to the creative flow of the subconscious can be a shock to the psyche and has the potential to be both unbalancing and unhealthy. For all of Picasso's genius, he is, I think, an example of someone who opened himself up a little too quickly to the creative flow of his own subconscious.

So, if you're just (re)embarking on a journey of creative self-discovery, my advice would be to take it slowly. You have a lifetime of creativity ahead of you. Treat yourself as a new bud about to flower, and give nature the time it needs to help the beautiful flower inside you unfold into its full creative glory.

5

"Eureka" Talking: Giving Voice to Inspiration

The physicists at the Bohr Institute called it "talking to one another so we can find out what we do and don't know, in order to learn what we need to know."

Nobel Prize–winning physicist Murray Gel-Mann, in an interview with Bill Moyers on PBS, revealed that he made one of his most important theoretical breakthroughs when he made a mistake in presenting a mathematical description of an event in a lecture and suddenly realized that this "mistake" was not a mistake at all, but held the key to solving a problem in physics he had long been contemplating, but for which he had never found a satisfactory answer.

Dr. Jean Houston, in her audiotape "Awakening the Brain," described an experience as a young girl with Edgar Bergen and "dummy" Charlie McCarthy. Houston's father, who wrote comedy skits for Bergen, had to drop off a script and invited his daughter to come up and meet Bergen in his dressing room. The door to Bergen's dressing room was open, and Houston and the young girl walked in. Bergen had his back to the door and didn't hear them enter. Incredibly, Bergen was actually talking to Charlie, asking him everything from the meaning of life to the structure of the universe—not exactly questions for a dummy.

Houston became uncomfortable eavesdropping on Bergen and Charlie, and he coughed to make his and his daughter's presence known. Bergen turned around and, somewhat embarrassed, said, "You caught me." When Bergen regained his composure, he explained somewhat sheepishly to Houston and his daughter that it was the strangest thing, but when he asked Charlie questions, he always got answers—answers that were always unexpected, and occasionally profound!

What do the physicists at the Bohr Institute, Murray Gel-Mann, and Edgar Bergen have in common? They're all practicing the creative technique of "discovery through verbalization." By having the courage (and trust) to allow the "talking part of themselves" (as contrasted, say, with that more silent part we know as our thoughts) to offer up ideas, they were all able to discover things they "didn't know they knew," things that, in theory, must have been inside them all along, but which, had they not been said, might very well never have been heard.

If you've ever brainstormed a business problem with a co-worker and found yourself somehow coming up with a truly amazing idea that literally just popped out of your mouth, then you know about this power of creative verbalizing, or "eureka talking," as I like to think of it. It is at once powerful, magical, surprising, humbling, and wonderfully self-affirming.

I remember once consulting with a client who was looking for a name for her exposition marketing and promotion firm. In our conversation, I suggested that as a naming strategy, we look at the word *exposition* and try to combine part or all of it with another "benefit-oriented" word root.

"How could you do that?" she asked.

"Well," I said without really thinking, "maybe we could use the word *exponential* somehow. We could call the company Exponential Marketing, visually break up the word *exponential* to resemble a mathematical exponent, and use the tag line, 'marketing raised to its highest power.'" Eureka! There it was: name, logo concept, and tag line, born effortlessly! No creative struggle, no creative angst—just magic.

■ ■ ■

Morey Amsterdam (the wisecracking Buddy on the old Dick Van Dyke Show) was once asked to write jokes for John F. Kennedy's presidential campaign. In a meeting with Kennedy, the two got to talking about Kennedy's tendency to pause to think for several seconds before answering interviewers' questions. It's hard to imagine that thinking before one speaks could be a liability, but in Kennedy's case it was. People perceived his delay in responding as a lack of decisiveness. Amsterdam's recommendation: "Simply start talking. The answers will be there."

There is a sense here of not overanalyzing, of joining the "just do it" school of creative thought (or would that be creative *talk?*) without second-guessing oneself. It's allowing what wants and needs to be said at any moment in time, to be said. It's allowing your intuitive self to speak without letting your analytical or judgmental self get in the way. Essentially, it's telling the truth, your truth. And, as you might imagine, it takes a great deal of courage, trust, and self-confidence to do it. After all, there's always the chance that you'll say something absurd, foolish, or embarrassing, isn't there?

How might you begin opening up the channel to your intuitive genius to let it have its say? Two suggestions:

■ Free-associate with a tape recorder. Set aside fifteen minutes a day, and talk about everything and anything that comes to mind. Tell stories. Describe your childhood. Make things up. If you're at a loss for words, begin describing things around the room, including ideas as to how you might improve them. Just keep talking. You'll be amazed at what comes out. (With time, you may even discover your "voice," as writers call it.)

- Force yourself to speak in metaphors and analogies by constantly using the word *like* (or *as*). Example: Picking up loose garbage is a lot like—what? "Packing the guts back into a cadaver"? "Licking the street with your nose"? "Serving throw-up at a picnic"? Writing a novel is like—what? I once heard *Sophie's Choice* author William Styron say, "It's like crawling from Moscow to Vladivostok on your knees." Adding *like* or *as* to your sentences forces you to (1) start creating analogies and metaphors, which is terrific training for the creative mind anyway, and (2) start eureka talking. Chances are you will not have a metaphor or analogy in mind, so you'll have to create one on the spot. You may find yourself, initially, at a complete loss for words, but eventually you'll find yourself, because of the pressure to complete the sentence, saying some truly remarkable, fun, and often funny things.

■ ■ ■

Does this pressure to say something on the spot help or hinder the eureka talking "training" process? I've been somewhat surprised to discover that the pressure does indeed seem to help. When you are forced to come up with an answer, invariably you do. You have no other choice. Let me give you three examples from my own experience.

Several years ago, I was asked to give a "creative talk on creativity" to members of a new-age religion. I agreed to do the talk pro bono, with the understanding that I be allowed to experiment and try something new. I wanted to test my own eureka talking abilities in a highly stressful situation: presenting in front of a live audience.

My idea/challenge: to try to create an "invention to order" for someone in the audience. As part of the challenge, I asked that an audience member pick an object, any object, that he or she would like me to base my "inventions" upon. A kindly old gentleman obliged and held up a pencil.

"An edible pencil for kids, a pencil that fits on your finger, a pencil that has a word counter (like a pedometer), an 'artistic' pencil that looks like a Salvador Dali clock, a body art pencil, a 'liquid pencil' that highlights the pencil's conventional lead markings with colorful marker outlines, a pencil with a thin roll of paper attached." Forty-some pencil "inventions" later they stopped me and agreed that I had indeed won the challenge. Frankly, I was a bit surprised I had pulled it off, and even more surprised that there were actually one or two ideas that seem to merit further investigation and development—quite possibly even patents. As Morey Amsterdam said, "Simply start talking, and the answers will be there."

A similar but unplanned experiment happened on my Connecticut cable show, "Meet the Inventors." My guests were three toy inventors from the Norwalk, Connecticut, invention and design firm Thin Air. Among their inventions that we talked about was Elmo the Heavenly Elf, a character that the inventors had been commissioned by Pepsi to create for a special Christmas promotion. My question to the inventors: "Why couldn't I, or anyone else for that matter, just come up with some crazy concept and name for a character and go out and license it ourselves?" Good question, and as the interviewer I should have stopped while I was ahead—but no, for some reason I added the phrase, "You know, a character like . . ."

So there I was, with a live student audience, taping a show (that would not be edited) for a quarter of a million potential viewers and having to come up with some stupid character concept in a split second of air time. "You know, a character like, uh, well . . ."

I was desperate, and so without thinking I just blurted out, "A character called . . . Gravel Voice, who speaks like this," and I made a suitably strange gravelly voiced explanation of the character. Not great, but not bad either: Gravel Voice could be one of a whole line of characters, each with some kind of special effect tied in with its name (Thunder Breath, Lightning Legs, "Buzz" Tickerhead, etc.).

The last and most bizarre experiment in eureka talking happened as a kind of dare from business associate and friend, Bob Sharp. Bob, a fan of WNBC radio in New York City, was listening one afternoon to Alan Colmes's afternoon talk show. Alan invited famous people to hawk their newest ware—book, video, sitcom, movie, whatever. On this particular day, though, Alan was in trouble. It seems that some important somebody couldn't, at the last minute, make it, and so Alan was stuck with a whole lot of dead air time to fill. "Friend" Bob called and, unbeknownst to me, offered the services of an afternoon guest who would "create ideas, on the spot, for interested callers."

Well, strangely enough, Colmes said yes. And so Bob and I jumped in a car for the forty-five-minute drive to New York City. Colmes got ex-pitcher, author, and inventor Jim Bouton to fill in until "the mystery guests from Connecticut" arrived. Once again, despite the pressure of several hundred thousand listeners, I was surprised to find that eureka talking actually worked. I started talking, and incredibly the ideas followed. Most of that afternoon is a blur, except I do remember one idea I came up with for the wife of an unemployed photographer.

"Why not," I said, "have your husband create a book of photographic puns, or visual photographic jokes?" Both she and host Colmes loved the idea.

▬ 6 ▬

Creative Dreaming: Finding a "Dream" Solution

In the 1950s, when my late father, J. Clarke "Matti" Mattimore, was working in advertising, one of his most successful creations was a contest for Pepsi. The idea was to have people call up their local radio station and be recorded saying Pepsi's tag line. The radio station would play these recordings over the air, and if a person recognized his or her own voice, he or she could call up and win a prize. Surprisingly, it was harder to win than you might think. People, it turns out, have trouble recognizing their own voices.

To make the contest work, the Pepsi brass felt they needed a compelling tag line for the people to record. My father worked and worked on the line, but came up dry. It wasn't until he slept on it that he got the answer. In a dream, his subconscious (presumably) suggested having the people say, "Say Pepsi, Please!" Short and sweet. Memorable. It even had the alliteration of the two *p*'s going for it. What made it a truly inspired line, though, was that it was a classy alternative to the then well-known phrase, "Gimme a Coke!" The "Say Pepsi, Please!" contest became the most successful radio contest ever run up to that time.

What's always intrigued me about this story was that my father got the answer to his problem in a dream. This seemed to me like the best possible way to be creative: all the results with none of the work.

Using dreams to creatively solve problems is not that uncommon. The idea for Dr. Jekyll and Mr. Hyde came to Robert Louis Stevenson in a dream. The Russian chemist Mendeleyev "saw" the periodic table of elements in a dream. James Watt got the idea for manufacturing shotgun pellets when he saw them falling like rain in his dream. The idea: Let molten lead, like rain, fall through the air to form the pellets.

The question that intrigued me was, How can one harness the power of dreams for creative inspiration? In the early 1980s, I began experimenting with trying to invent new games in my dreams. My method was to try to imagine, before going to bed, what a new game might feel like.

Sometimes, too, I'd ask my subconscious what it would like to invent. My results were mixed. I did ultimately get from my dreams a viable new game (a new kind of three-dimensional tic-tac-toe) that was patentable, but that I was never able to license. I was most disappointed, however, with the process. Seemingly, dreaming was not something that could be controlled. Sometimes it worked; most times it didn't. The process was as unpredictable as Mr. Hyde's personality.

Fast forward to the late 1980s. Without consciously trying, I had a story come through in a dream that I now see as a metaphor for the process, and potential, of dreaming itself. I'd like to share it with you.

I call my dream story "The Genius Dome." The genius dome is a large domelike structure (dropped off by aliens?) filled with special brain-stimulating gases. When we earthlings enter the dome, we are transformed into geniuses, presumably able to use the 90 percent of our brain power that psychologists tell us we're not now using. As soon as we leave the dome, however, we instantly go back to being "10 percenters," our old, nongenius selves. This basic story idea could form the basis for a science fiction short story, a novel, a play, or even a movie comedy. The story's dramatic conflict and creative tension would come from the geniuses inside the dome trying to take their genius with them to the outside. Maybe even, in a bit of irony, a child could be the one to provide the answer.

I think of this story idea as a metaphor for the dream state itself because our dreams can be a source of genius for us. But as with the genius dome, we have to figure out how to get the genius out of our dreams and into the real world. Or do we?

The Hidden Benefits of Creative Dreaming

Research indicates that we benefit from our dreams even when our dream recall is zero. Laurence Cruz discusses a fascinating study to support this claim. In sleep lab research with students in an intensive language class, it was found that "those who showed more rapid eye movement (REM) or dream sleep were those who learned the fastest, while those whose REM sleep remained at normal levels did not do so well in class." Cruz goes on to say that "the experiment suggested that dreaming plays an important role in processing information even when we recall no dreams. There may also be a clue here as to how 'sleeping on' a problem or decision often produces a neat solution even when we don't remember our dreams."[1]

So what's the answer? My conclusion is that we *can* have it both ways.

Whether you're conscious of working within the genius dome of your dreams or not, you can still realize the benefits of creative dreaming. You do not necessarily have to have the dramatic revelations in your dreams that Descartes and Beethoven, Kekule and Howe, Milton and Blake had. Your answers may come in more subtle ways, meaning that they may not even come while dreaming at all. Thanks to work you may have unknowingly done while you were asleep, an answer may present itself during the day as a "gut feeling," or hunch. Or maybe you'll see something, or someone will say something, that triggers an association with a forgotten dream event that somehow contains your answer.

■   ■   ■

There are two simple keys to working with your dream state in this way. One is that you must learn to speak the language of dreams—the language of metaphor and symbol, of intuition and hunches.

Second, simple as it may sound, you must use the tool that you've been given. To keep your dreaming subconscious mind functioning at its highest efficiency (so that you can rely on it when you need it most to solve a real-world problem), you must continually give it problems to solve. If need be, set daily or weekly idea goals for yourself when you're first starting out. The only way you'll come to know and trust your subconscious dreamer as a valid problem solver is if it has actually solved problems for you in the past. Ultimately, with time and a few successes, you won't even question it. You'll just come to expect success.

You might wonder how my successful dream work today differs from the only marginally successful game invention dream work I did more than ten years ago. There are really only two differences. The obvious one is that I know now, from years of trial and error, that I can rely on the subconscious dream mechanism to solve problems for me. I trust the process. Positive expectations do seem to yield positive results.

The other difference is that I've come to redefine how I view the dream state and how and where it might provide me with answers. I know now that although most of the creative work will be done by the subconscious during sleep and dreaming, the answer may or may not come in a dream. This realization has made me much more alert to "waking dream" solutions that may appear—often magically—in my real-world life. Again, it may be something someone says, or an object I see, or even an ad on television that contains the answer.

I mentioned before that we need to learn to speak the language of dreams. A key theme and goal of this book is to demonstrate the power and potential of metaphors for creative problem solving in business. Let's turn now to an exercise to help you consciously generate creative problem-solving metaphors.

A Dream Exercise

Because of the ethereal and individual nature of dreams and dream inter-pretation, it seemed like an impossible challenge I had given myself: I wanted to invent a dream exercise for my seminars that could (1) demon-strate the symbology of dreams and its potential for solving a real-world business problem and (2) at the same time give the student the satisfac-tion of "getting the right answer." The problem is that dream images mean different things to different people, and therefore do not lend them-selves to a right-or-wrong answer exercise.

As always, though, there was a solution to my seemingly impossible challenge. Instead of showing people how to *interpret* their dreams, I'd show them consciously how to *create* them. After all, we all create dreams anyway. We're just not awake when we do it, and therefore we're not conscious of the process. By *consciously* creating our own dreams, we can become more aware of the process (and language) of dreams, and ulti-mately its potential for solving real-world business problems.

Here's how we do it in the seminars: I give out creative business case studies, ones that have already been solved in a very innovative way. Then, I have each person create a dreamlike story (using dream images, symbols, and metaphors) that somehow communicates the case study's innovative solution. Here's an example:

In *The Wall Street Journal* on December 19, 1989, there was a front-page story about Coke's efforts to penetrate new markets worldwide. The article mentioned a particularly difficult international marketing problem in Indonesia that had been solved in, I thought, a very creative way. It seems that the favorite national drinks in Indonesia, when Coke showed up, were tea and tropical fruit juices. The Indonesians had not tried car-bonated beverages in general and Coke in particular, and did not particu-larly like them when they did. So, what's a marketer to do?

See if you can guess the solution to the problem from this "dream" I created:

■ ■ ■

> I was in a dark pool of water in the jungle. The dark water started bubbling up, a lot like a lava pool might. Somehow, I knew the pool wasn't dangerous, but the local people weren't convinced; they had a superstition about it.
>
> To calm their fears, I tried giving the natives some of the dark water to drink, but they wouldn't take it. In fact, they became even more afraid, and started building a wall of tropi-cal plants and fruits to separate me and the dark, bubbling pool of water from their village.

I climbed over the wall, and saw the local witch doctor dressed in a British uniform drinking tea.

The witch doctor got mad when he saw me looking at him. So he took fruit from the wall and started to stuff it into little glass bottles. Then he warmed the bottles over a fire until the fruit started melting and bubbling, and threw the bottles at me. (The bottles resembled a kind of home-made Molotov, or in this case "fruit," cocktail.) I was afraid the bottles would blow up in my face. Before they did, though, I woke up.

What was this dream trying to tell me?

■　■　■

The real-world solution to Coke's marketing problem was what you might call a phase-in marketing approach. Coke executives realized that they needed to accustom the Indonesian palate to carbonated drinks. And so, as an interim step, Coke first introduced strawberry, pineapple, and even banana-flavored soft drinks. Eventually, Coke expects the Coca-Cola brand to surpass the local-flavor soft drinks because "over time, palates search for a less sweet taste."

Did you figure it out? Did my consciously created dream capture the essence of the solution?

Want another example? Let's say you're trying to invent a new kind of computer, one that works on a different principle entirely from the electronic, silicon-chip-based platforms of today. You start having dreams about armies carrying piles of data, sometimes colliding with one another. Then finally you have a dream about armies marching into one another, but this time with no collision. Does this give you any ideas?

It did for Alan Huang, Bell Labs researcher and creator of this dream. Huang realized that laser beams, like the opposing armies, could pass through one another unchanged. This led to the invention of the first viable optical computer, an invention that some researchers consider to be "the most important breakthrough in computers since the invention of the microchip."[2]

Notes

1. Laurence Cruz, "Listen to Your Dreams," *Creative Living*, Winter 1993, Vol. 31. Published by Northwestern Mutual Life, Milwaukee, Wis.
2. George Land and Beth Jarman, *Breakpoint and Beyond* (New York: Harper Business, 1992), p. 157.

Section Two

Exercising Your Creativity

7

Those Crazy Inventors: A Creative Warm-Up Exercise

Imagine yourself in a room full of strangers, where it's your job as the facilitator to help them brainstorm new ideas. These people don't necessarily want to be there. They may not think of themselves as particularly creative, and indeed may be afraid of "creativity." They even may not particularly like or trust the other people (their co-workers) with whom they're supposed to brainstorm. So what do you do?

How can you (1) help make the people feel comfortable and even begin to trust one another, (2) take the "creative pressure" off them, (3) show them that it's okay to fail—in fact, that it's critical to the process that they do fail, and (4) if possible, get them laughing, or at least smiling? And do all this in ten minutes or less with a warm-up exercise?

Let's consider the subject of *chicken fishing* as a theoretical basis for our exercise.

Have you ever been chicken fishing?

Thomas Edison went once. And he even landed a "big one." This happened when he was a young boy (before he left school full time to be tutored by his mother). Edison dangled a baited line outside his upper-floor schoolroom window, and did indeed catch a chicken in the school-yard below. His classmates were delighted, his teacher less so.

If you study the lives of great inventors, two key personality traits stand out: a fierce independence and persistence. You get a sense of Edison's fierce independence from the anecdote above. But what about persistence and its natural corollary, failure? How might they be related to a creativity warm-up exercise?

Read most history books on inventors, and you'll learn the story of the inventor's success(es). Oh, yes, there may be some brief mention of the failures that led to the success, but never in any great detail. Why? For one thing, an inventor's failures invariably outnumber his successes, and editorial space being what it is, who's got room for the thousands of experiments that *didn't* work? More important, who (especially in

America) wants to read about failure? We're interested in how someone succeeded, not how they failed, right?

The problem with focusing just on the successes is that we get a biased view of the process. We're not shown that most often, inventing (or life, for that matter) is really about failing. This, of course, is why persistence is so important.

Invariably, creative people will tell you that they learn more from their failures than from their successes. Indeed, Thomas Edison even took issue with calling his failures "failures." He preferred to think of them as invaluable contributors to the eventual success of the project, helping him to learn what wouldn't work. You can imagine the "learning" that took place in the testing of 60,000 substances that led Edison and his team to the successful invention of the alkaline battery.

Personality trait number two is fierce independence. Challenging the status quo takes great courage and self-confidence. An extension of this courage is the inventor's willingness to entertain ideas that others consider radical or just plain crazy. Think again of Edison and his chicken fishing experiment. Great success, it seems, comes only to those willing to risk great failure and great embarrassment. Alexander Graham Bell, you're trying to talk through a wire? Right. You want to "send invisible pictures through the air" to a windowed box in someone's home, Messrs. Zworykin and Farnsworth? Listen, don't call me, I'll call you.

If failure, and the attendant willingness to risk thinking about seemingly very far out or even absurd ideas, is so important to the invention process (and by extension to a successful brainstorming session), why not, I thought, create a creativity warm-up exercise that champions both? And why not do it with history's greatest inventors? What better role models could there be?

So here it is: a multiple-choice test that I hope will help you (and your brainstorming buddies) not take yourself so seriously and make "failing," if not fun, at least a valued learning experience. In each of the twelve multiple-choice questions, one of the answers (believe it or not) is actually true. See if you can guess which one.

A Creative Warm-Up Exercise

1. As part of his grooming regimen, Henry Ford would:
   a. Add particles of sand to his toothpaste to increase its abrasive tartar-removing qualities.
   b. Dye his hair with rusty water.
   c. Keep the balls of his feet soft by applying a coating of his own saliva to them nightly.

2. Thomas Edison proposed to his second wife by:
   a. Recording the marriage proposal on his newly invented phonograph and playing it during a candlelight dinner.
   b. Tapping out the proposal in Morse code, from his hand to hers.
   c. Making a movie of himself proposing on bended knee.
3. Because he thought it would benefit his health, Ben Franklin would:
   a. Walk barefoot through the mud, believing it helped stimulate the eight vital organs of the body.
   b. Drink water only from a glass container that had been left out in the sun for hours.
   c. Take "air baths" by sitting naked in front of an open window and inhaling deeply.
4. Nikola Tesla, who invented the alternating current (AC) motor, once tried to invent a device that:
   a. Diagnosed people's health by electronically reading their auras.
   b. Elicited memories when applied to various parts of the head.
   c. Photographed thoughts on the retina of the eye.
5. George Eastman, inventor of the Kodak camera:
   a. Was a supporter of the thirteen-month calendar.
   b. Took a photograph of himself every day from age thirty-one to seventy-two.
   c. Invented a camera that when swallowed by cows took pictures of each of their four stomachs.
6. As a health precaution, Alexander Graham Bell:
   a. Covered his ear with gauze every time he used the telephone.
   b. Covered the windows in his home to block out the rays of the full moon.
   c. Drank his own urine.
7. Edison was convinced that:
   a. The Germans were using a "thought ray" during World War I to control President Wilson's mind.
   b. There were submicroscopic entities, or "little people," living in his brain.
   c. He would someday invent a pair of "electronic goggles" to see into the future.
8. Vulcanized rubber inventor Charles Goodyear:
   a. Considered making rubberized water beds for the ill.
   b. Proposed that newspapers be printed on rubber.

(continued)

    c. Foresaw rubber parasols, rubber carpets, rubber blackboards, and even rubber bank notes.

    d. All of the above.

9. Milkman Gail Borden:

    a. Had his tomb built in the shape of a condensed-milk can.

    b. Tried to sell condensed cow's blood as an ingredient in a salad dressing.

    c. Filled a public pool with milk to promote the idea that milk baths were good for the skin.

10. Charles Hall, who invented a practical way to produce aluminum, theorized that:

    a. A daily diet of seaweed could cure asthma.

    b. Aluminum eyeglass frames would enable the wearer to better predict the weather.

    c. Tobacco had snuffed out creative impulses during the previous 200 years.

    d. All of the above.

11. Alexander Graham Bell:

    a. Tried to get his dog to talk by teaching it to growl as he manipulated its mouth.

    b. Charted the vibrations of his own voice on a piece of smoked glass by talking into a mounted ear with a piece of hay stuck into it.

    c. Recommended that aspiring inventors reflect a smell and measure its velocity of transmission.

    d. All of the above.

12. Hating unnecessary suffering, Rudolf Diesel once invented:

    a. An ammonia bomb that would confuse the enemy instead of killing him.

    b. An adhesive-wire fence as an alternative to barbed wire.

    c. A bog-creating mud plow to trap soldiers in the mud instead of shooting them.

Answers:
1, b; 2, b; 3, c; 4, c; 5, a; 6, b; 7, b; 8, d; 9, a; 10, c; 11, d; 12, a.

■ ■ ■

How'd you do? If you didn't score particularly well, don't feel bad. I tried this test on members of the Inventors Association of Connecticut, and they didn't score as well on it as a group of gifted seventh graders. Some people get a little frustrated with this test. That's because there's really no way to logically deduce the correct answer. So, in a sense, you have to do just what the inventors did: risk great failure by voting for a choice that potentially could make you feel a little foolish.

Again, it's important to let ourselves entertain wild and crazy ideas if we ever hope to arrive at that truly revolutionary, breakthrough idea. If during a session someone feels more likely to suggest an idea that is foolish or crazy because of the example set by Edison, Ford, or Bell above, then this creative warm-up will have been worth its weight in ideational gold.

In the best creative sessions, you'll find it comes down to not taking yourself too seriously if you're serious about creating great ideas.

8

Idea Hooks®: A Moments-of-Inspiration Exercise

In Part One, I described how I came to discover the creative theory of invention called Idea Hooks. You can imagine the excitement I felt when I investigated the thought processes and "eureka moments" of history's greatest inventors and discovered that my Idea Hooks theory was correct. It was indeed true that in literally hundreds of instances, it was a concrete, physical object that provided the stimulus for the inventor's creative breakthrough. And this was not true only for famous inventors. Lesser-known inventors used Idea Hooks as well. Take English inventor Alastair Pilkington, for example, who in the late 1950s was trying to invent a way to manufacture better, smoother, less costly glass. His Idea Hook was a film of fat floating in his wife's dishwater. The idea: Float molten glass on a layer of melted metal to provide an otherwise unachievable smoothness.

Or how about Sir Marc Isaac Brunel? He was trying to invent a way to construct more efficient underwater tunnels. His Idea Hook was a shipworm tunneling through a timber. He noticed that as the worm tunneled forward, it constructed a self-contained tube for itself. Brunel built a mechanical imitation of the living model: His patented shield is a "short steel cylinder which is pushed forward (like the shipworm) by mechanical means as work progresses. Without this huge boring machine, river tunneling would have been next to impossible."[1]

Or consider the imaginative English doctor Peter Roget, best known for his writing of *Roget's Thesaurus*, first published in 1852. It was Roget who discovered what historian Daniel J. Boorstin calls the motion picture phenomenon. His Idea Hook was a cart. "One day as he [Roget] looked out through the Venetian blinds in his study, he noticed that the cart moving through the street seemed to be proceeding by jerks. He suspected that it was a series of stationary impressions joined together that gave the eye the impression of a cart in motion. In 1824, he offered the Royal Society his paper on 'Persistence of Vision with Regard to Moving Objects.' So casually he had noted what would make possible the motion pictures."[2]

Of course, in most cases, it wasn't the Idea Hook per se that led to the inventor's breakthrough. The Idea Hook was the stimulus for the breakthrough because it embodied a principle that when applied to the inventor's problem provided a solution. Obviously, though, for the Idea Hook to work, the inventor first needed to have an in-depth knowledge of the problem he was trying to solve and, as important, be sensitive to and have a talent for seeing the inherent principles in the things around him.

It's as if the right-brain, holistic mind has a built-in, principle-matching antenna, and when the right Idea Hook comes along, the intuitive mind immediately recognizes it, a light bulb goes off, and the inventor has the eureka experience that supplies the long-searched-for answer.

So the underlying key to success with the Idea Hook technique is an ability to recognize principles and ultimately transfer them through the holistic and primarily intuitive right brain. How good at holistic principle recognition and transfer are you? Here are a dozen multiple-choice questions to test your skill. I've selected some of history's greatest inventions and mixed their Idea Hooks (the ones that led to the actual discoveries) with a few "creative" alternatives. See if you can guess which Idea Hook led to which discovery.

Before you begin, however, a word of advice. You may find that trying to answer these questions using a logical and analytical, left-brain way of thinking is very difficult indeed. As a rule, *none* of the answers seem to make much sense. I'd recommend instead, therefore, that you try first to make an intuitive judgment about the correct answer. In other words, start by picking the answer that feels right. After that, then (and only then) you can let your analytical mind try to figure out logically why your choice may or may not be the correct one.

The advantage of this intuition-first, analysis-second approach is that even if you don't get the right answer, you'll still have had the experience of trying to holistically principle match, which is what this exercise is all about anyway. That and, of course, having some fun.

Moments-of-Inspiration Exercise

1. When Dr. René Laennec was looking for a way to help him diagnose the health of his patients, what incident provided the inspiration for his invention of the stethoscope?
   a. A beret being tossed in the air by one of his neighbors
   b. Children sending signals to each other by tapping on either end of a log

(continued)

    c. A medical colleague chewing his lunch loudly with his mouth wide open

    d. A woodpecker pecking on a tree outside the hospital

2. Samuel Colt's inspiration for his famous six-shooter revolver was

    a. The Big Dipper

    b. A pitchfork he threw into the side of a barn

    c. A ship's wheel

    d. The musical score for "Amazing Grace"

3. John Dunlop got the idea for rubber tires from:

    a. His garden hose

    b. A molted snake skin

    c. A raincoat

    d. A sugar maple tree

4. Henry Ford conceived of a better way to mass produce his cars from a visit to:

    a. A slaughterhouse

    b. A supermarket

    c. A tobacco farm

    d. A graveyard

5. Rudolf Diesel got the idea for the design of his diesel engine from looking at:

    a. A magnifying glass

    b. A typewriter

    c. A da Vinci drawing of the human lungs

    d. An Aztec spear

6. Samuel Morse conceived of the telegraph relay system when he saw:

    a. A snake slithering in the grass

    b. A drawing of women sporting lightning-rod hats in Europe during the 1820s

    c. Fresh horses being substituted for tired horses at relay stations

    d. A dog barking up a tree at a cat

7. Charles Duryea got the idea for the spray injection carburetor when:

    a. He saw his wife spray herself with perfume using a perfume atomizer.

    b. He took a walk in the London fog.

    c. He saw a special mining machine pulverize a piece of iron-rich ore.

    d. He visited a waterfall in Belgium.

8. Thomas Edison got the idea for the first multiplex telegraph by considering the workings of:
   a. The Gatling gun
   b. His pocket watch
   c. A mechanical piggy bank
   d. A water pump
9. Maxim's inspiration for the design of the gun silencer was:
   a. A whistle
   b. The whirlpool effect of water flowing down the drain of his sink
   c. A fireplace bellows
   d. A lobster trap
10. Eli Whitney realized that he'd be able to invent a simple cotton "gin" (short for engine) when he saw:
    a. A cat reach through a fence trying to grab a chicken
    b. A waterwheel
    c. A stagecoach
    d. His landlord scraping a frying pan with a thin metal spatula.
11. The de Montgolfier brothers conceived of the first hot air balloon when they saw:
    a. Burnt paper scraps rise above the flames in their chimney
    b. Stained glass windows blow out of a burning church
    c. A friend faint from inhaling cigar smoke on a bet
    d. A blowfish for the first time at a Paris fish market
12. Carrier got the idea for the air conditioner when he:
    a. Took a steam bath at the Yale Club in New York City.
    b. Bought a completely sealed Japanese glass terrarium.
    c. Saw water condensing on the side of a glass.
    d. Choked on a piece of ice.

Answers:
1, b; 2, c; 3, a; 4, a; 5, d; 6, c; 7, a; 8, d; 9, b; 10, a; 11, a; 12, c.

Notes

1. W. J. J. Gordon, "Discovery by Analogy," *Chemtech*, March 1980, p. 168.
2. Daniel J. Boorstin, *The Creators* (New York: Random House, 1992), p. 740.

9

The Source Mind: Looking for "Essential" Relationships

When Teddy Roosevelt decided to run for President, one of the first things he did was take a course in mathematics. Why?

When I first got out of school and worked at a New York ad agency, I shared an office with a very bright account executive named Moira Hearne. Moira had been an undergraduate history major and had gone on to take her MBA at Wharton. Since I didn't go to business school, I was curious to know what she felt was the most valuable thing she had learned at Wharton. I was surprised by her answer. "With the history major, my mind was able to kind of float around—move from subject to subject without a whole lot of focus," she said. "But business school changed all that. The math in particular forced me to become much more precise and disciplined in my thinking. The best thing about business school was that it really sharpened up my mind."

Sounds a little like John Houseman's line as Professor Kingsfield in *The Paper Chase,* "You come in here with minds filled with mush, and leave here thinking like a lawyer!" doesn't it?

Lawyer, advertising executive, even President—I am convinced that with the right mental disciplines and training, most of us can learn to do things we'd normally presume to be impossible. Yes, talent is important. Inspiration is critical. Love is essential. But so is hard work. And creativity, despite what the Muses might have you believe, is no exception.

My experience with most successful inventors is that they work very hard at their craft; hard to the point of obsession. The reason: Inventors (and certainly other creative people as well) never know when, and under what guise, inspiration will arrive. So their antennas are always up (or out), ready to receive some inspired transmission from the gods that contains the answer to their problem.

Actually, though, this is only half the story. The best inventors don't just stand by waiting patiently to receive a flash of inspiration. No, they actively seek out inspiration. How? By following three of the most important mental disciplines that I know for inventing—or any other creative pursuit, for that matter: (1) continually asking all kinds of questions, no matter how far out or seemingly absurd, (2) trying to visualize or "see" answers, and (3) freely associating different concepts, no matter how remote the connections. All three are creative mental disciplines that can be developed and honed to a very high level of proficiency.

Happily, developing and practicing these creative disciplines is a lot more fun than taking a mathematics, law, or even business school course. (For a discussion of the value of creative questioning, see the Gray Box Exercise, page 52. For examples and instructions on developing the ability to visualize answers, see Image Streaming, page 92.)

It's this third area, the ability to associate seemingly very different concepts, that deserves some attention here.

Developing the Source Mind

In the simplest of terms, creativity is about making connections between two or more seemingly unrelated things or ideas. Okay, fine. The question is, how, specifically, do you do this? One way is by developing, as financier Bernard Baruch said of Edison, a "source mind." What's a source mind? A source mind, naturally enough, is one that traces things back to their source by trying to make very few assumptions, by continually asking the question why or how, and by being willing to entertain unconventional explanations when conventional thinking or approaches are found to be lacking.

Another feature of the source mind is that because it is constantly tracing problems and their apparent causes back to their roots, the source mind thinker becomes proficient at identifying "problem essences": underlying principles and patterns, and relationships based on cause and effect.

If one has as a basic belief that there is an essential unity to the universe, and that somehow everything is related to everything else, then the ability to discover these relationships, especially among seemingly unrelated phenomena, is not only the basis for great creative accomplishments, but also, it seems to me, an underlying characteristic of true genius.

■ ■ ■

P. Ranganath Nayak and John M. Ketteringham give an intriguing example of the source mind at work and the relating of seemingly unrelated phenomena.

Question: What does the produce section at your local supermarket have to do with manufacturing a better, more cost-effective car? Indeed, how did one man's thinking about American supermarkets lead to a theory that, without exaggeration, literally revolutionized American manufacturing in the 1980s?

Answer: It was Kiichiro Toyoda, founder of the Toyota Motor Works, who in 1935, two years before the first Toyota car was ever produced, compared the automobile assembly line to an American supermarket:

> He noticed that in an American market, great quantities of food—much of it perishable—are gathered. It can't be stored on site, because the store doesn't have the space and can't afford the cost of storage, and because much of the food would spoil in storage. So, as shelves empty in the store, the staff notes the need for more supplies; the supplier is informed and the bread, or hams, or fresh peaches arrive "just in time." If this system could somehow be translated to auto production, Kiichiro thought, the elimination of waste, the elimination of parts warehouses, and the greater coordination of all production stages could reduce costs dramatically. It would give the company that made it work a significant competitive advantage.[1]

Of course, it did give Toyota a significant advantage, until American manufacturing rediscovered "just in time" manufacturing for itself—some might say just in time.

Want some practice in source mind thinking? See if you can discover the surprising connections between the seemingly unrelated elements in the following questions.

■ ■ ■

Question 1: How might the invention of the Delco car battery in 1911 have added to the American woman's "drive" for equal rights?

Question 2. Before the introduction of firearms, why was bowling considered a threat to national security in England?

Question 3: Why did George Marsh predict, in the early nineteenth century, that the invention of the silk hat would cause the formation of many lakes and bogs in the United States? (Hint: This has nothing to do with the silkworm.)

Answers:

1. The Delco battery enabled women, for the first time, to drive alone, since they did not now need the help or strength of a man to crank-start the car.

2. Bowling was considered a threat to national security because men would bowl instead of practicing their archery skills.

3. With the invention of the silk hat, Marsh guessed correctly that there would be reduced demand for beaver furs. Since fewer beavers would be killed, greater numbers of beavers could once again set about their business of building dams, resulting in the creation of more lakes and bogs.

How'd you do? Let's try another one.

■ ■ ■

It's the 1830s. You are with Charles Darwin aboard the *Beagle,* and you decide to go ashore with him in Madagascar. As a naturalist, he's fascinated by the exotic plants. You're wondering what's for lunch. Darwin sees a white orchid with an extremely long nectar spur, measures it, and discovers that the spur is almost a foot long. You think yes, it's unique, but nothing to write home about. But you can see by the expression on Darwin's face that he is intrigued.

Question: What's bothering Darwin? What question is he asking himself? What does Darwin ultimately predict exists as a result of seeing this flower?

Answer: The question that Darwin asked himself was how such a flower could be pollinated. He surmised that there would have to exist some kind of insect with a foot-long "nose" or beak to pollinate this flower. You, like his contemporaries, think Darwin has been aboard ship a little too long and ridicule him for his theory. As it turns out, though, Darwin has the last laugh. Some twenty years later a nocturnal moth is discovered in Madagascar that has a wingspan of only five and a half inches, but that (you guessed it) has a proboscis a foot long. In honor of Darwin's feat in predicting its existence, the insect is named *Xanthopan morganii praedicta.*

Developing the source mind by continually asking how or why is a key to creative greatness. It is as useful in a corporate marketing department, a regional sales office, or an MIS department as it is in an inventor's laboratory.

Let's try one more.

■ ■ ■

You own a fifty-foot sailboat, which you anchor in the harbor of your yacht club. You spend most of your weekends sleeping aboard the boat because it feels like taking a vacation without actually going anywhere. Each weekend you plan to sleep in, but you notice that for some reason you seem to need less sleep when you stay overnight on the boat than when you sleep at home.

Question: What's the reason? Might there be an invention here?

You surmise that there are four possible explanations: (1) the fresh air, (2) less stress because it's the weekend, and therefore a need for less sleep, (3) less or different kinds of noise, or (4) something else (the one that actually led to a new invention). Can you guess what it was?

Answer: New York inventor Jerome Murray decided that it might be the rocking of the boat that made him require less sleep. An interesting hypothesis!

Assignment: The next step is to design a marketable product to capitalize on this theory. Any ideas?

Answer: What Mr. Murray did was to design four small, identical electromechanical boxes to replace the casters on the legs of his bed so that he could be rocked to sleep at home. The invention worked, and Mr. Murray had that much more time at home to invent other things.

■ ■ ■

Want other problems to get your source mind going? Start by looking around your office. Ask yourself why you can't read the ruler. Or maybe you'd like to know why you can't cut a perfectly straight line more than four inches long with your scissors. Or why is it that you can't find that guy's name in your Rolodex (did you file him under his name, his company, or his occupation?)?

If you trace each of these questions back to its source of design, you'll have your answer, and quite possibly be on the road to a new invention.

Note

1. P. Ranganath Nayak and John M. Ketteringham, *Breakthroughs* (New York: Rawson Associates, 1986), p. 212.

10

Fermi Problems: Guesstimating in Today's Decimal-Point World

Several years ago, I was interviewing candidates for a part-time secretarial/administrative job with my company. It wasn't long before I grew tired of the standard "what experience do you have?" kind of questions and decided to try something a little more fun. What I came up with was a one-question quiz to show me how resourceful a thinker this new hire might be. Here it is:

You are on your $3 million yacht on your way home from a long weekend visiting a friend in the Philippines. Your navigator has just informed you that you are over the deepest point in the Pacific Ocean, the Marianas Trench. One of your clumsier guests is admiring a twelve-pound cannonball that you recently salvaged from a sunken sixteenth century Spanish galleon. Mr. Clumsy accidentally drops the cannonball over the side. How long does it taking for the cannonball to reach the bottom of the ocean?

Before reading this further, please try to solve this problem, paying special attention, if you will, to *how* you tried to solve it.

What did you do? Did you make a completely wild guess because "there simply wasn't enough information to solve the problem"? Did you get overly bogged down in the details, asking yourself about, say, the salinity or temperature of the water, because you wanted to get the "exactly right" answer? Or were you able to zero in on the two most important components of this problem, namely, how deep is the Marianas Trench, and how fast might a cannonball fall through the water; hazard a guess as to what the depth of the Trench and the speed of the cannonball might be; and then, most important, be willing to "guesstimate" an answer?

It was disappointing to me that most of the candidates (and friends

I later tried this one) simply made a wild guess, without in any way trying to figure out what the correct answer might be. It's as if they couldn't be 100 percent right, there was no use in trying to be 95 percent right. It was the exception when someone was actually willing to risk an approximation. The broader implication is that it's more important to get the right answer than it is to learn how to think. By the way, the Marianas Trench is approximately 5.7 miles deep, and a cannonball will drop at a rate of almost ten feet per second. So it will take the cannonball approximately 63 minutes to reach the bottom of the Trench.

How many burgers does your local McDonald's serve in a day? How many thousands (or is it millions) of words can you write with one Bic ball-point pen before it runs out of ink? What percentage of the times do you say *I* instead of *you* in conversation?

Commonsense Guesstimating

These are all examples of what most physicists will recognize as a Fermi problem. Enrico Fermi won the Nobel Prize for his work in elementary particle physics, and four years later, under the squash courts at the University of Chicago, produced the first sustained nuclear reaction, which of course led to the development of the atomic bomb. Fermi invented "Fermi problems" as a way to help his physics students learn to think for themselves. What makes a Fermi problem unique is that unlike most brain twisters or logic puzzles, a Fermi problem does *not* have contained within it all the information you need to solve the problem. Fermi recognized that in real-world physics, as in life, there are many situations where the information we might want or need to solve a problem is simply not available. So, as with the Marianas Trench example, you're forced to simply make a guess. The key, though, is learning how to make an educated guess.

In many ways it's also like writing a business plan, which we'll get to shortly. But first we need to know how many piano tuners there are in Chicago.

Believe it or not, this was actually a question that Fermi posed to his students at the University of Chicago. How did he recommend that they solve it? By having the courage to make some educated guesses and assumptions.

- How many people live in Chicago? 3 million?
- How many people per family? Say an average of four.
- How many families own pianos? Fermi guessed one out of three (I might have guessed one out of five or six).

▪ This would mean, then, that there are approximately 250,000 pianos in Chicago.

▪ How often would each piano be tuned? Say once every ten years?

▪ This means there are 25,000 tunings per year.

▪ How many pianos can a tuner tune in a day? Four?

▪ Then 4 times 250 working days per year means that each piano tuner could tune 1,000 pianos per year.

▪ So with 25,000 tunings available, this would mean that there should be approximately 25 piano tuners working at any one time in Chicago, which, as it turns out, if you look in the Chicago Yellow Pages, is pretty close to the actual number.

Why did this work, even though obviously it is only an approximation? The law of averages is partly responsible. At any point in the process, you can make incorrect assumptions, high or low. This is to be expected. In fact, you'll probably make several wrong assumptions, both high and low. But because of the law of averages, your incorrect assumptions will, on the whole, balance out because half the time you'll assume high and the other half of the time you'll assume low.

What does this have to do with business and/or creativity? A great deal. Often, when we are on the trail of a breakthrough idea, we need to solve problems that have never been solved before and base decisions on information that simply does not exist. In a world where we increasingly rely on outside authority for our answers, from what foods we should eat to how to raise our kids, the creative businessperson must retain the right and the ability to think for herself. She must question the "experts" at every turn by using her own experience, intuition, and common sense. The ability to guesstimate quickly and accurately will become an increasingly valuable and necessary business skill as the rate of business change continues to accelerate. There is simply no longer the time, money, or staff to make sure of all your decisions. The creative businessperson must be able to tolerate, and indeed thrive in, an increasingly ambiguous and chaotic business world. Your best guess will often be the best you can do.

▪ ▪ ▪

Suppose, for example, you've been asked to write a marketing plan for a new phone add-on device that at the touch of a button will send your name, company, address, and telephone number to a visual display—or better yet, a "phone message printer"—on another person's phone. In addition to conventional outlets like mass merchandisers and electronics stores, you'd like to know the number of "phone stores" in the United States. Unfortunately, this figure is not available, either from market research houses or from the U.S. government. What do you do? One solution would be to simply go to your local library, pull out a few phone directories from around the country, turn to the Yellow Pages, and start counting. You could then guesstimate how many stores there were nationwide based on the number of stores per 100,000 people in each of your "counted" cities. (This, by the way, is exactly what one of my marketing consultant friends did for a large telecommunications client.)

Often if you can break a difficult problem down into smaller, manageable ones, you can figure out a way to solve it.

■ ■ ■

Quiz 1: Why would the Nobel Prize–winning physicist Enrico Fermi have torn up a sheet of notebook paper and thrown the pieces over his head exactly at the moment when the world's first atom bomb went off in 1945 at Alamagordo, New Mexico?

Answer: It was Fermi's "quick and dirty" way of measuring the blast of the atomic bomb. As it turned out, the pieces were carried about 2 1/2 yards behind him, and Fermi was able to calculate, based on this distance, that the atom bomb's energy was equivalent to that of ten thousand tons of TNT.

■ ■ ■

Quiz 2: How did Ben Franklin determine which of his different-colored clothes absorbed the most heat and which of his different-colored clothes reflected the most heat? (You probably already know that black absorbs the most and white the least, but what about other colors in between?) Design a simple experiment to find the answer, Hint: It's wintertime, but not too cold.

Answer: Ben Franklin conceived of an ingenious experiment to test the heat absorbency/reflectivity of a given color. He simply took "samples of broadcloth" of various colors and laid them on the snow on a bright sunshiny morning. "In a few hours," reported Franklin, "the black, being warmed most by the sun, was so low as to be below the stroke of the sun's ray's; the dark blue, almost as low, the lighter blue not quite so much as the dark, the other colors less as they were lighter, and the quite white remained on the surface of the snow, not having entered it at all."

His conclusion: "May we not learn from hence that black clothes are not so fit to wear in a hot sunny climate or season as white ones? That all summer hats, particularly for soldiers, should be white, and that garden walls intended for fruit should be black."

One of my favorite experimenter stories comes from Weston, Connecticut, inventor Stan Mason. A key element of Stan's invention strategy is to identify emerging trends and then invent a new product that satisfies a human need that this new trend might create. A great example of this inventive strategy was Stan's development of his line of microwave cooking dishes, Masonware, in the late 1970s. A dramatic rise in the percentage of working mothers combined with the growing penetration of microwave ovens in U.S. households spelled opportunity to Stan. Why not create a line of cooking dishes designed specifically for the "unique cooking environment" in a microwave oven? Great idea! But to be more than just hype, this new line of cooking ware needed to be substantively different from conventional cookware. Theoretically it should both be easier to use and do a better job of actually cooking the food.

Could the cookware somehow position the food in the most advantageous position for cooking? Quite possibly. But, of course, this required knowing where the "best" microwave rays would be when the oven was on, and what their intensity would be.

■ ■ ■

Quiz 3: Design a simple experiment to find the microwave oven's "hot spots."

Answer: Stan and his development team put several plastic shelves of unpopped popcorn kernels in the microwave and watched to see which kernels popped first. When they had discovered the pattern of the oven's hottest rays (they didn't pop in the corners or at the very center: The shape looked much like a mushroom cloud), they designed the cookware to fit this pattern—and cook the food most efficiently. This was an elegant, nontechnological solution to a problem that with less ingenuity would have required sophisticated scientific testing equipment.

11

The Gray Box Technique: Asking the Right Questions

I'd like to invite you to a creative training session and have you follow along as I, and members of the audience, try an exercise that I invented several years ago called the Gray Box Technique. I use the Gray Box Technique for three main reasons: (1) to give seminar attendees a direct, "minds-on" experience imitating the thinking processes of great inventors, (2) to demonstrate the value of asking good questions, and (3) to show people that they know a lot more, and are much more creative, than they might ever have imagined. This exercise has the potential, literally, to change forever the way you view your creative ability. If you think of yourself as "not particularly creative" before this exercise, you just might change this self-limiting view to something just short of "creative genius" after the exercise.

Are you skeptical? Let's see what happens.

■ ■ ■

Imagine that you are with a room full of people, and you've been invited to try the Gray Box Technique with the other audience members. I'm at the front of the room; I reach into a big white laundry sack and take out a shiny gray box about the size of a hatbox. I place the box on the lectern in the front of the room for all to see.

Inside this box is one of my game inventions that never made it to market. So it's a game invention you could not have either heard of or seen before. There's no possible way that you could know what's inside this box, right? What I'd like to do now is play Twenty Questions with you. See if you can guess what's inside the box by asking simple yes/no questions. That's all there is to it! Shall we give it a try?

Oh, by the way, before we start, I don't want to put any undue pressure on you, but I've done this exercise with fourth graders, and they got the answer!

Okay? So who's got the first question?

These are the actual questions, as they happened, in the order they were asked by an audience of business professionals in Stamford, Connecticut, on June 21, 1991.

Is there a board in the game? **No.**
Is there a ball? **No.**
Are there pieces? **Yes.**
Are there dice? **No.**
Are there cards? **Yes.**
Do you have to put it together? **Yes.**
Can it be played by more than one person? **Yes.**
Is there a winner? **Yes.**
Are they ordinary playing cards? **No.**
Do you win by luck alone? **No.**
Do the cards have pictures on them? **Yes.**
Do they form something when they're put together? **Yes.**
Is it a puzzle? **No.**
Are the cards rectangular? **Yes and no. Some are. Some aren't.**
Are there more than cards in there? **Yes.**
Do you wind up with a three-dimensional thing? **Yes!**
Do the pieces determine your ability to get a card and play a card?
   No.

■ ■ ■

Are there additional pieces used to put the cards together to make them stand up in the three dimensions? **Yes.**

Does the structure have cards in it? **Yes.**

Is the structure sort of a frame that you would slide cards into to make a picture? **Yes.**

Is it like a rack? **No.**

You said some of the cards were rectangular. Are there other shapes as well? **Yes.**

Is it a slot thing? Like a mail box slot? Does it take skill to get the cards through a small opening? **No.**

Are all the players trying to make the exact same structure? **Good question, but no.**

Once the cards are put in, can they be moved around within the frame? **No.**

Is each player making his or her own construction? **No.**

Do all the cards have to be used up before the game is over? **No.**

Is the purpose to form a completed picture? **Partially, yes.**

Do you try to obstruct your opponent in putting the cards in? **Yes.**

Is speed an issue? **Not really.**

Are you building up like a skyscraper or maybe more free form? **Yes.**

Are there words on the cards? **No.**

Are there colors? **Yes, as part of the pictures there are colors.**

Do you assemble the cards with different colors on each card? **No.**

Are both sides of the cards important? **Not after they're played.**

Is it designed to be a fun game as opposed to a test? **Yes.**

Is the structure predetermined? **Good question. No, it's not.**

Is the objective to use up all the cards? **No.**

Are there notches in the cards—to put them together? **No.**

Is there scoring? **Yes—well, there are winners and losers.**

Do the players have specific roles in constructing whatever it is they're constructing? **Great question—yes, that's important!**

Will the structure be different each time the game is played? **Yes.**

Can your opponent remove the cards? **No; once they're played, they're played.**

■ ■ ■

Is each player trying to create a separate, distinct part of the structure? **No.**

Do the cards have directions or words on them? **No.**

Is there a structure you're trying to complete—are you using the designs on each card to create a final structure? **Yes.**

Is it a travel version of a Lego set? **No.**

Can a person win by having more cards in their structure? **No.**

Does each card have as its picture only part of what could be put together? **Yes, that's correct, very good!**

Do you have to play the cards in a specific order—play some cards before other cards? **Yes.**

Is each player trying to form a different structure? **Yes.**

In order to reach your goal state, do you need to use the cards that your opponent has played? **Yes, you do. (The "goal state"—I like that phrase; I've never heard that before.)**

Is the object of the game as you're putting these cards together, do the cards have patterns such as lines or pathways where you're trying to get to your side of the table to the other side of your opponent? **No, but not a bad idea.**

Are you creating visual images here? **Yes.**

■ ■ ■

Is one player trying to build one visual image or structure while the opponents are trying to build other, different structures? **Yes! You've got it!**

So everybody has different shapes that they're trying to create.

Everybody has different cards, and nobody knows what other people are trying to create, right? **Yes.**

Is each player trying to build more than one structure at a time? **Yes!**

So, what, everybody has, say, five different structures that they're trying to create with these cards? The first one to create all the structures wins? Is that the game? **Yes, yes, yes! That's it!**

You got it. Congratulations. You and the group asked only fifty-some questions—and you came up with the right answer. Or did you?

The truth is, I've misled you in this exercise. Yes, there actually was one of my game inventions in the box, but as you'll see, *I wasn't responding to your questions about the game* inside the gray box. Instead, I was simply answering your questions randomly—making up my yes and no responses as we went along. I could as easily have said yes to there being a board in the game (see question 1) as no. I could as easily have said no to there being cards in the game (see question 5) as yes. The game evolved into what it ultimately became based on the combination of my (semi-) random responses and your questions. The truth is that *you* created the construction game *by virtue of the kinds of questions you asked!*

Now admittedly, there was some skill in my facilitation of this exercise. I had to keep track of my yes and no responses and be consistent. But I had no preconceived notion of where the exercise would go or what invention we'd ultimately create. In fact, every time I facilitate this exercise, we end up with a different invention, some of which are quite good and a few of which are extraordinary! The fourth graders, for instance, came up with a very different idea for a card game, a kind of symbolic matching/biography game of famous people. On one side of the card they'd have a picture of say, a strawberry; on the other side a picture of baseball player Darryl Strawberry. On one side of the card a heart; on the other side, a picture of Gary Hart. A cute idea. (Think of cards for Red Buttons, Sally Field, or even George Bush.)

Staying With the Problem

Let's look at some of the ramifications of the Gray Box Technique. For one, it shows in a dramatic way the power of creative and continued questioning. If we train ourselves not to give up, to continue to ask questions, as we did with the Gray Box Technique, we will find a solution to our problem. Every successful inventor I've ever known (close to 200 around the world) has told me that he or she was able to persist in solving a difficult problem when others had given up because, as with the invention in the gray box, he or she "knew that the answer was there." To them, as to Sir Isaac Newton who said he made his world-changing discoveries "by constantly thinking upon them," it was simply a matter of staying with the problem until they found the answer—or, in some cases, the answer found them. It gives Edison's 99 percent perspiration, 1 percent inspiration quote a whole new meaning, doesn't it? Seemingly, an inventor's "perspiration" consists primarily of continued and creative question asking.

Another interesting dynamic of the Gray Box Technique is what I call the "evolving visual." With each new question and yes or no answer, we saw the invention evolve into something different right before our minds. The content of the questions asked, and the ensuing answers, constantly forced us to change our mental image of what the invention might be. We might even have had some preconceptions of what the invention was, which had to be changed as a new question showed our preconception to be incorrect. If we could have looked inside the mind of an Edison or Newton, I suspect we'd have seen a similar evolving visual phenomenon taking place there as well.

■　■　■

A corollary of the evolving visual phenomenon is what I call the desire for synthesis. Each step of the way, we tried to synthesize the new information we learned from our questions into a viable, integrated whole. Since our evolving visual of the game was incomplete, we were, in psychological terms, looking for closure, a way to complete the incomplete image in our minds. The only way we could do this was by trying to *synthesize* all we had learned into a new and unique whole. And we know, of course, that the desire for synthesis is a hallmark of the inventive mind.

Finally, there was certainly an element of ongoing experimentation in the Gray Box Technique. We kept at our question asking because we knew the answer was there. But to do this, we had to continually search for new "experiments" (that is to say, new questions) that we could "run" on our evolving, incomplete visual. Like any great experimental scientist, if one thing didn't work, we tried something else until we started to get results that began to make sense, or were at least interesting. At some point, we probably even tried a rather far-out idea "just to see what would happen." The Gray Box Technique allowed us to conduct a simple form of what Einstein called "thought experiments."

And by the way, do you know what Einstein said was the key to his success? It was because, as he put it, he "never stopped asking questions."

◼ *Section Three* ◼

Inventive Role Models: The Creative Techniques of Creative Genius

▬ *12* ▬▬▬▬▬▬▬▬▬▬▬▬▬▬▬

Disney and the Lightning Bug

If you could travel back in time and meet anyone from history, whom would you chose: da Vinci, Einstein, Edison, Freud, Newton, Benjamin Franklin, Mozart, Jesus? And if you really could meet one or more of history's greats, what would you ask them? Probably you'd be interested in knowing what and how they thought—essentially, how they came up with their ideas.

Let's imagine for a moment that you've been sent back to fifteenth-century Italy to work for Leonardo da Vinci, ostensibly as his gofer/apprentice. Really, though, you're there as a reporter for *Time* magazine. Your editor at *Time* wants you to discover, through insightful questioning, how da Vinci's mind works. Specifically, your editor wants to know how da Vinci was able to imagine such so-far-ahead-of-their-time inventions as the spring-driven car, the helicopter, and the parachute. The hope, then, is that when you return to the present, you can share da Vinci's "strategies for genius" in your soon-to-be-published Pulitzer Prize-winning article, "My Year with da Vinci."

What questions might you ask the great maestro? And what would you do if when you asked da Vinci how he came up with his ideas, he simply kept saying, "I don't know—they just sort of come to me"?

In a very real sense, Robert Dilts, cofounder of the Dynamic Learning Center in Ben Lomond, California, has taken on just such an assignment. By studying the original writings of great geniuses through history, Dilts has attempted to give us a time machine of sorts into the ways these great thinkers thought. To date he has written monographs (ranging in length from 20 to 150 pages) on the thinking strategies of such greats as da Vinci, Einstein, Mozart, Disney, Jesus of Nazareth, electronics inventor Nikola Tesla, Aristotle, Freud, and even Sherlock Holmes (Sir Authur Conan Doyle).[1]

How did Robert Dilts go about analyzing the thinking patterns of history's greats? And what specifically did he discover? Finally, how can the reader apply these findings to help solve today's business problems? Let's find out.

The Strategy for Unlocking the Strategies of Genius

Robert Dilts is one of the pioneers of neuro-linguistic programming (NLP), on which he has written five of the seminal books.[2] NLP is a modeling/process technology that attempts to find out how the brain (neuro) works by analyzing language patterns (linguistic) and nonverbal communication. The goal is to make explicit maps (or programs) of the successful thinking strategies of people with special talents, such as da Vinci, Disney, or Einstein. Specifically, NLP explores the way we use the fundamental mental abilities of sight, hearing, and feeling to organize and perform in the world around us.

We start by "making the fantasy real" with Walt Disney.

Walter Elias Disney: Making the Fantasy Real

There is a wonderful anecdote about Walt Disney that illustrates several of his unique strategies of genius. Just before opening the Pirates of the Caribbean ride at Disneyland, Disney was touring the ride and felt strangely dissatisfied. In his heart he felt that something was missing, although he couldn't quite put his finger on what it was. He gathered as many employees as he could find—including the maintenance and food service personnel—and led them through a kind of sensual "tour de *focus*."

"Does it look right?" he asked. Yes, the costumes and shrubbery were authentic; the buildings had been copied from the New Orleans French Quarter down to their intricate wrought-iron decorations. They all looked right.

"Does it sound right?" Disney had had the latest in audio equipment installed to accurately reproduce the sounds of music, voices, boats, and even animals that you'd associate with the Caribbean. Yes, it sounded right.

"Does it feel right?" He had controlled the temperature and humidity to exactly match that of a sultry New Orleans night. Yes, it felt right.

"Does it smell right?" An elaborate smell-producing system had been created that could combine the smells of Cajun food with gunpowder, moss, and brine. Yes, it smelled right. And yet something was still missing. What was it, Disney asked.

Finally, one of the young men who had been sweeping the floors said, "Well, Mr. Disney, I grew up in the South, and what strikes me is that on a summer night like this there ought to be lightning bugs." Disney's face lit up. That, of course, was it! The young man was given a generous bonus, and Disney actually had live lightning bugs shipped in until he could figure out a way to imitate them mechanically.

Attention to detail? Following your intuition? Integrating diverse points of view? Getting the best out of your people? Let's take a look at Robert Dilts's analysis of Disney to see what strategies of genius this anecdote (and others) suggests.

Essentially, there are three strategies that embody the fundamentals of Disney's extraordinary creativity and problem-solving methods: (1) use of all the senses, (2) break "large" problems or creative tasks down into smaller and smaller manageable pieces (and levels), and (3) adopt the "view of the other." Disney's modus operandi for achieving these three strategies was to allow himself to be three different people in one. As one of Disney's co-worker put it, "there were actually three different Walts [and] you never knew which one was coming into your meeting."[3] Robert Dilts has labeled these three different Walts "the dreamer, the realist, and the critic." All three are important to contributing to the entrepreneur's ultimate success. Let's see how.

Walt: The Dreamer

Walt took his dreaming very seriously. As one associate put it, "When Walt was deep in thought he would lower one brow, squint his eyes, let his jaw drop, and stare fixedly at some point in space, often holding the attitude for several moments. No words could break the spell."[4] Based on an NLP analysis of Disney's body postures and writings, Dilts has theorized that Disney was engaging in an important psychological process known as synesthesia, which means literally a synthesizing of the senses. Synesthesia occurs when someone overlaps two or more senses, as when one feels what one sees, or sees images of sounds that one hears. (Consider, for example, Mozart, who said about composing a piece of music, "and the whole, though it be long, stands almost complete and finished in my mind, so that I can survey it, like a fine picture or a beautiful statue at a glance."[5] Similarly, Disney wrote in the introductory notes to his film *Fantasia*, "When I heard the music it made pictures in my head . . . here are the pictures."[6])

How can you combine the senses to make your visions more real or profound? Try involving *all* the senses. If you're brainstorming a new children's game, bring out some modeling clay to involve the sense of touch in possible new game ideas. If you're writing a marketing plan, consider organizing it like Beethoven's Fifth Symphony and including a dramatic and powerful opening few lines. If you're giving a speech, try to paint pictures with your words.

Walter: The Realist

Pretend for a moment that you've been asked to invent a device that will let you analyze, in incredibly fine detail, the physical actions of a character you'd like to animate. Each second of character movement will need to be broken down into twenty-four separate drawings because there are twenty-four frames per second in a motion picture. What kind of device might you invent to assist you in this process? P.S.: Your "budget" for inventing this device is less than a nickel. Any ideas?

It is said that one of the tricks that Walt Disney used to help him break down each second of screen time into twenty-four separate drawings was to first draw his characters on rubber bands. Then he could slowly stretch and move the different body parts of the character (and get ideas on how to draw them most authentically) by simply pulling and stretching the rubber band in different directions.

This ability to break down his vision—or the creative task, if you will—into pieces (and levels) small enough to make them manageable or doable was the essence of Disney the realist. Disney might start by picturing basic scenes. Then he'd picture the specific actions that made up those scenes. And finally, he'd picture minute movements that made up each of those actions.

To help him in this process of developing progressively finer detail, Disney invented the creative presentation technique we know today as storyboarding. Storyboarding is a visual table of contents that can be used to represent key events in virtually any creative process. Storyboarding has been used by George Lucas to chart his Star Wars pictures, by all major advertising agencies to present proposed TV commercials, and in brainstorming sessions to visualize and categorize key concepts as they are created.

Storyboarding is an especially effective tool for process reengineering work. By helping to visualize the process, it makes it easier to find steps—and possibly parts—in any complicated manufacturing process that can be eliminated. You can even use storyboarding to help you structure a more dynamic training seminar or speech.

Disney: The Critic

If the dreamer can come up with the ideas and the realist can figure our how to make the ideas real, then it's the critic that has the final word on whether the ideas are any good. To be a truly effective critic of anyone's work, but especially of one's own, requires a great deal of psychological distance. You have to be able to get far enough away, as Disney put it, to view whatever it is you're working on objectively. Paradoxically, it seems that one of the techniques that Disney used to successfully achieve his psychological distance as the critic was also the key to his success as both the dreamer and the realist, namely, "taking on the role of the other."

Disney could take on the role of the other by becoming his characters. As one of his associates put it, "Mickey's voice was always done by Walt, and he felt the lines and the situation so completely that he could not keep from acting out the gestures and even the body attitudes as he said the dialogue."[7]

Obviously this total identification with his characters served him well in the dreamer and realist phases of any project. But what about the critic phase? Wouldn't such total identification get in the way of objectivity? Yes, had it not been for Disney's ability to simply take this ability to become the other and transfer it to becoming "another other," the audience. Like the best salespeople, Disney could look at what he was selling from the client's (the audience's) point of view.

Here's what Disney had to say about his process. (Notice that he says *he*, not *I*.)

■ ■ ■

He should get *far enough away* from his story to take a *second look* at it . . . to see whether there is any dead phase . . . to see whether the personalities are going to be interesting and appealing to the audience. He should also try to see the things that his characters are doing are of an interesting nature.[8]

■ ■ ■

"Far enough away" is an important statement here. It implies the feature of psychological distance talked about earlier. For the creative businessperson, this psychological distance can be achieved in two major ways: through adopting the role of the other as Disney did so as not to take criticism of "your baby" personally, or by making time work for you by leaving a project for a time and then coming back to it. The age-old recommendation to "sleep on it" can be especially important to the successful work of the critic. If you can't sleep on it, simply taking frequent breaks during the course of a project will help the critic in you achieve the psychological distance it needs.

The other important feature of Disney's statement was his recommendation to take a second look. This second look can provide you with important information that you might leave out if you look from only one perspective. Metaphorically, you might think of this second look this way: If you're viewing something with just one eye, you'll perceive only what's on the surface, but if you can look at something with both eyes, you'll be able to perceive depth as well—as Disney did.

Dreamer, Realist, Critic—Finding a Place for Them Within Yourself

The projection room where Disney would judge how successful his animators were in translating his fantastic visions into animated reality came to be known by his artists and writers as the "sweat box." To cultivate the roles of dreamer, realist, and critic in yourself, why not create environments (physical or otherwise) much like the Disney "sweat box" where each of these three distinct personas can tell you what it thinks.

What might a room dedicated especially to making the dreamer feel at home look like? Posters of far-away or imaginary places, comfortable chairs, running water?

How about the realist? A room filled with his or her tools of the trade? Computers, drawing tables, reference materials?

And the critic? Maybe a room would include posters saying, "We're not criticizing you when we criticize one of your ideas," or "Check your ego at the door," or "We make ideas stronger by finding their weakest points." Maybe you even put a large chain at the entry to the room with the line, "Where's the weakest link?"

■ ■ ■

Before you scoff at this idea of physically separating these different problem-solving personas, consider the inventing style of the world's most prolific inventor, Dr. Yoshiro NakaMats. (NakaMats holds over 2300 patents, more than double the number held by the next most prolific inventor, Thomas Edison. For instance, NakaMats invented the floppy disk and licensed it to IBM.) As Charles "Chic" Thompson explains, Naka-Mats has three different rooms for three different parts of the creative process. He calls room 1 the "static room." It's a place where he goes for complete peace and quite, in order to free-associate. It's here that he lets his mind wander. The room is filled with only natural things, like a rock garden, running water, wood, and plants. There is no metal or concrete.

Room 2 is his "dynamic room." It is "dark, with black-and-white striped walls, leather furniture, and special audio and video equipment." In the dynamic room, NakaMats listens first to jazz, then to easy listening, and finally to Beethoven's Fifth Symphony, which for him "is good music for conclusions."

Finally, room 3 is a swimming pool, where he does "creative swimming" and comes up with his best ideas. "I have a special way of holding my breath and swimming underwater," he says. He records these ideas with a special Plexiglass writing pad that lets him write under water.[9]

Of course, if you're not ready to create three separate "innovation rooms," you might start by using a less expensive creative thinking strategy invented by creativity expert and author Dr. Edward DeBono. De-Bono recommends using different colored hats to isolate different thinking styles: a black hat for the critic, a red one for a feeling or emotional point of view, a green hat for creativity, etc.[10] Next time you're starting a new venture, why not bring along several "hats of different colors" to make sure the dreamer, realist, and critic inside of you all get a chance to be heard!

Notes

1. Robert Dilts, *Strategies of Genius* (Cupertino, Calif.: Meta Publications, 1993).
2. Robert Dilts, J. Grinder, R. Bandler, J. Delozier, *Neuro-Linguistic Programming*, Vol. 1 (Cupertino, Calif.: Meta Publications, 1980).
3. F. Thomas and O. Johnson, *Disney Animation: The Illusion of Life* (New York: Abbeyville Press, 1981), p. 379.
4. Ibid., p. 85.
5. E. Holmes, *The Life of Mozart Including His Correspondence* (London: Chapman & Hall, 1878), pp. 211–13.
6. J. Culhane, *Walt Disney's Fantasia* (New York: Harry N. Abrahams Inc., 1981), p. 29.
7. Thomas and Johnson, p. 77.
8. Ibid., p. 367.
9. Charles Thompson, *What a Great Idea* (New York: Harper Perennial, 1992), pp. xiii–xiv.
10. Edward DeBono, *Six Thinking Hats* (Boston-Toronto: Little, Brown and Company, 1985), p. 32.

13

Leonardo da Vinci: *Sapere Vedere*— Learning How to See

When Leonardo da Vinci was still an apprentice, his father, Ser Piero, gave him a shield and asked him to paint something on it. Leonardo decided to paint something that would "terrify the enemy." For this purpose, Leonardo carried to a room "lizards, newts, crickets, serpents, butterflies, grasshoppers, bats and other strange animals; out of these he formed an ugly monster, horrible and terrifying, which emitted a poisonous breath and turned the air into flame."[1]

When his father came to pick up the shield, he "received a great shock" and almost fell over backwards with fright. To Ser Piero, the thing appeared "nothing short of a miracle."[2]

Strategy of Combination

Leonardo used a similar "strategy of combination" to make imaginary animals out of real ones. Da Vinci's biographer Vasari reports: "On the back of a most strange lizard, found by a vinedresser of the Belvedere, Leonardo attached wings made of scales taken from other lizards, held by quicksilver, which as the lizard moved, quivered with the motion. He then made it eyes, a horn, and a beard, tamed it and, keeping it in a box, he showed it to friends to make them flee for fear."[3]

The idea of combining nature's creations in imaginative ways is reflective of a profound da Vinci strategy of genius. Look at the mechanical inventions in his notebooks, and you can't help but think that da Vinci used the same strategy for imagining these inventions as he did for creating imaginary animals, namely, to identify "universal forms" and then combine these forms in new and useful ways.

For Leonardo, the gateway to discovery of and insight into these universal forms was direct observation and experience. In fact, he often signed himself "disciple of experience." And his primary tool for uncovering the universal forms and processes behind the results of nature's creations was something he called *saper vedere*, "knowing how to see."

The Internal and the External

There are two main components, one of which could be thought of as external, the other internal, of da Vinci's "knowing how to see" process. The first involves learning something visually, by heart; the second involves using one's "common sense," as da Vinci calls it (in today's terms this would mean using both the conscious and the subconscious mind), to capture the deepest essence of the thing mentally. Once this has occurred, the object under study becomes available to the mind as a usable, combinable universal form from which new inventions can be imagined. Let's look at the "learning something by heart" component of the process first.

For da Vinci, to have learned something by heart meant that one had developed such a rich and detailed internal visual map of the thing or phenomenon that it was no longer necessary to make any reference to the original to reproduce it, either in one's mind or on paper. For da Vinci, the only way to learn something by heart was by first learning how to draw it accurately.

How? da Vinci suggested using the following method:

■   ■   ■

> When you have drawn the same thing so many times that it seems you know it by heart try to do it without the model; but have a tracing made of the model upon a thin piece of smooth glass and lay this upon the drawing you have made without the model. Note well where the tracing and your drawing do not tally . . . return to the model in order to copy the part where you were wrong so many times as to fix it in your mind.[4]

■   ■   ■

Being able to draw something accurately was, however, only a means to an end for da Vinci. When the thing could be reproduced at will, then and only then could the common sense (the sense that judged and integrated the perceptions of the other five senses) begin to work faithfully with the now-internalized object. Through the common sense the "deepest essence" of the learnt-by-heart thing would be revealed until finally one arrived at an appreciation of its universal form. This universal form could then be mentally experimented with and combined with other universal forms to create, as Leonardo put it, some of nature's "infinite causes which were never set forth in experience."

If you look at Leonardo's drawings of the human body, you get the feeling that they are more "real" and alive than any photograph could ever be. They are exquisite examples of "capturing the deepest essence of a phenomenon." They also reflect the depth to which Leonardo must have internalized and understood what he was representing in order to produce such powerful and true drawings. In fact, Leonardo did not call his drawings drawings at all; he called them demonstrations.

How can Leonardo's strategy of genius for learning how to see and ultimately discerning universal forms be of use to you, especially if you have no inclination to represent things visually? Leonardo developed three very specific techniques, which I call (1) the twilight technique, (2) the three-view technique, and (3) the subconscious trigger technique.

The Twilight Technique

The time just before falling fully asleep at night and just before becoming fully awake in the morning is known in psychological terms as twilight time. Da Vinci has this to say about this time:

■ ■ ■

I have proved in my own case that it is of no small benefit on finding oneself in bed in the dark to go over again in the imagination the main outlines of the forms previously studied, or of other noteworthy things conceived by ingenious speculation; and this exercise is entirely to be commended, and it is useful in fixing things in the memory.[5]

■ ■ ■

If you wish to discover the deepest essences of problems to be solved (how, for instance, form intersects with function in a complex piece of machinery, how each system or part contributes to the whole of a complicated manufacturing process, or even how work patterns and responsibilities relate and add value to a company's overall vision), twilight time would seem to be a most opportune time to make these discoveries. By simultaneously giving you access to the logical, conscious mind's abilities and to the more fanciful wishes of the subconscious mind, twilight time can literally give you the best of both worlds.

Certainly, for anyone looking to develop a more powerful *visual imagination* ("the central guiding element/mental ability" in *all* the geniuses Robert Dilts studied), twilight time would seem to be the easiest and most productive time of day to develop it.

The Three-View Technique

If you've seen the anatomical drawings in da Vinci's notebooks, one thing is immediately apparent: Invariably, he would draw something from at least three different perspectives—from below, from above, and from the side(s). He did this, he says, because he wants "you to be left with a true complete knowledge of all you wish to learn of the human figure."[6]

Essentially, then, what da Vinci is saying is that until you have perceived and mapped something from a minimum of three different perspectives, you will not yet have a basis for understanding it. A "true complete knowledge" comes only from synthesizing these different points of view into a whole within the common sense.

So, consider trying to find a way to look at a problem from at least three different perspectives (think of Disney's dreamer, realist, critic strategy). Then, once you've identified these perspectives (contradictory though they may sometimes seem to be), try to integrate the essential elements of *all three of them* into one coherent whole. At the very least, you'll learn to identify and possibly appreciate another point of view; at best you'll attain a level of understanding and appreciation of your problem that will lead to a truly innovative solution.

The Subconscious Trigger Technique

In one of his treatises on painting, da Vinci has this to say about "stimulating and arousing the mind to various inventions": Stare at "walls spotted with various stains or with a mixture of different kinds of stones" until the mind starts to see in the shapes "a resemblance to various different landscapes adorned with mountains, rivers, rocks, trees, plains, wide valleys, and various groups of hills."[7]

Da Vinci goes on to say,

■ ■ ■

You will also be able to see diverse combats and figures in quick movement, and strange expressions of faces, and outlandish costumes, and an infinite number of things which you can reduce into separate and well-conceived forms. With such walls and different blends of stones it comes about as it does with the sounds of bells, in whose clanging you may discover every name and word that you can imagine.[8]

■ ■ ■

Much like a modern-day Rorschach test, this technique, da Vinci suggested, could be used as a way to tap into and exploit subconscious processes for creative ends.

So start with *unformed* stimuli to trigger unconscious creative processes. Cloud shapes. Spots on walls. Cracks in the pavement. Then with practice, you can train your mind to use *formed, everyday objects* to also trigger "unconscious" creative connections. An easy way to begin doing this is by simply squinting your eyes at things. This will make the formed object less precise, and make it easier for your subconscious mind to begin making creative connections and associations. Take, for instance, the concrete, everyday image of a bird in flight. By squinting your eyes at the bird, you might well imagine how to design a new kite, sculpt a more aerodynamic car, or invent a more "graceful" typeface.

An intriguing example of just such a connection occurred when Leonardo "discovered" that sound traveled in waves. He was standing by a well when he noticed a stone hit the water at the same moment a bell went off in a nearby church tower. His wrote in his journal:

■ ■ ■

The stone where it strikes the surface of the water, causes circles around it which spread until they are lost; and in the same the air, struck by a voice or noise, also has a circular motion, so he who is nearest hears the best and he who is most distant cannot hear it.[9]

■ ■ ■

Want to try the subconscious trigger technique right now? Squint your eyes at the letters on this page. What do you see? I'm seeing a group of super-intelligent intergalactic zoo animals leaping into my eyes, speeding down my optic nerve, and energizing my dormant brain cells into action. Now that these "letter animals" are let loose in my brain, I know that my thought processes will never again be quite the same.

I hope you'll find that the same thing can be said of your thought processes once you begin experimenting with da Vinci's subconscious trigger technique.

Da Vinci's Inventions

As with his anatomical drawings and works of art, it seems that da Vinci's primary motivation for creating inventions was to gain a deeper understanding of the world around him, and "nature's creations."

Essentially, da Vinci's inventions, and his motivations for creating them, can be categorized into four main types or areas:

- Devices common to his time that he studied for their unique elements and "essences" (clock mechanisms, foundry equipment)
- Devices common to his time that he improved upon by incorporating other mechanical principles into their design (the printing press, coin stamp, water mill, textile machines, and weapons)
- Experimental devices that he created to demonstrate fundamental theoretical principles of mechanics (friction devices, transmission gears)

- Original inventions based on his own theoretical ideas, arrived at primarily from his observations of nature (flying machines based on his observations of birds; streamlined ships based on the shapes of fish)

Common to all four of these strategies was, of course, da Vinci's ability to identify "nature's essences" by learning how to see. For the would-be inventor, engineer, or industrial designer (and even creative businessperson or entrepreneur), then, here is how you can adapt da Vinci's timeless formula for inventing:

- Make invention an ongoing mental exercise (dare I say life pursuit?) to identify key *features, elements, and essences* of any inventions (or systems) (past, present, or future) that you intuitively feel hold one of nature's "essential truths." (With the right point of view, you'll be hard pressed to find anything in this world that doesn't hold an essential truth of nature).
- "Internalize" these key features, elements, and essences by visualized repetition.
- Mentally, and in drawings, explore interrelationships of these key features by:
  — Combining them in a systematic way, and seeing what you get.
  — Looking at them from different perspectives (the three-view technique).

Notes

1. Andre Chastel, *The Genius of Leonardo da Vinci* (New York: Orion Press, 1961), p. 11.
2. Ibid.
3. Ibid.
4. Edward MacCurdy, *The Notebooks of Leonardo da Vinci* (New York: George Braziller, 1958), p. 877.
5. Ibid., p. 881.
6. Jean Mathe, *Leonardo da Vinci: Anatomical Drawings* (Crown Publishers, 1978), p. 26.
7. MacCurdy, *Notebooks*, pp. 873–74.
8. Ibid.
9. *Codex Atlanticus*, p. 1041 r.

14

Albert Einstein: Metaphors at Play

"Imagination is more important than knowledge."

"God does not play dice with the universe."

"Everything should be made as simple as possible, but not simpler."

Well-known quotes, all from the twentieth century's most widely acknowledged genius, Albert Einstein. One you might not be so familiar with, but which is essential for understanding Einstein's unique strategies of genius, was his oft-repeated statement, "Our thinking creates problems that the same type of thinking will not solve."

What did Einstein mean by this? And if the same type of thinking won't solve the problem (in physics, or any other field for that matter), what is the implied "different type of thinking" that will?

One of the well-known aphorisms in the field of creativity consulting is to "make the familiar strange." When we're overly familiar with something, we have all kinds of assumptions, biases, and preconceived notions that inhibit us from discovering new and potentially exciting ways of looking at it. By making the familiar strange, we can often once again look at that something with a fresh, new, almost naive perspective and open ourselves to the possibility of making some truly unique discovery.

Here' a simple example or test of how familiarity—and preconceived notions, assumptions, and/or biases—limits the scope of our creative thinking and problem-solving abilities:

> Which of the following numbers is most different from the others?
> 1) One
> 2) Thirteen
> 3) Thirty-one

Which number did you choose? If you're like most people, you probably assumed that the only numbers that applied to the question were the spelled-out numbers: "one," "thirteen," and "thirty-one." If so, you had a difficult time coming up with a viable answer. However, if you took an unbiased, "naive" view (almost as a child might) of the phrase "the following numbers" and included the notational numbers "1),", "2)," and "3)," then you certainly would have picked the number "2" because it is the only even number and has neither a "1" nor a "3" in it (as all the other numbers do). Because we're so used to seeing the numbers behind the parentheses as "not part of the problem" (serving only to enumerate the elements that are part of the problem), it is very difficult to break this assumption and view them as an essential element in the correct solution.

As in the example above, Einstein felt that language, powerful as it was for communicating abstract concepts, had the potential to be a "dangerous source of error and deception." To get beyond the inherent assumptions of language, and to keep the concepts and relationships "encoded by words and word-combinations" closer to the "world of impression," Einstein chose imagery and feelings as a way to conduct his most intriguing and productive "thought experiments."

Imaginary Constructions

- Riding through space on a light beam trying to see one's reflection in a mirror
- Having your feet tied to the bottom of an elevator that's being pulled through space by "imaginary beings"
- Living life in a two-dimensional world, and being one of the "flat beings with flat measuring rods" conducting experiments on infinity
- Viewing from above a blind beetle walking in endless circles on a large, seemingly flat sphere

These are the kinds of images that Einstein constructed in his mind as a way to question basic assumptions about the nature of "reality" and the universe. What makes these kinds of constructions so unique and potentially valuable, not only to a physicist, but also as a problem-solving strategy to the rest of us? There are three important features:

- They are visual in nature. By using visuals, Einstein was able to make the familiar strange and approach problems in physics with an entirely different mindset from those physicists who used primarily the "languages" of either mathematics or words. Visuals enabled Einstein to get an entirely different point of view.
- While constructed from many different elements, these images tend to be composed of common, everyday "memory pictures," as Einstein called them—objects that we can all identify with, such as trains, elevators, pebbles, beams of light, spheres, or mirrors. By using everyday

images, objects, and symbols, Einstein was using the concrete, visual language of the right brain, the same language that we all dream in.

- Einstein's constructed thought experiments allowed him (and others) to live the experience first hand because they were metaphorical pictures into which he could place himself with his imagination. By adding this extra feeling/role-playing element to the experiments, Einstein made his constructions that much more immediate and powerful. For a modern-day analogue, imagine the difference between designing your dream home using a virtual reality system, where the computer allows you to literally walk through your imagined house, and trying to visualize how your house will look and function by looking at blueprints drawn by your architect.

How can you create and use similar kinds of visual constructions to innovate better ways of doing things? Let's look at a real-world example of how to apply such constructions in business.

Good Evening, Lighthouse!

Imagine that you are an engineer working for a very bright project leader developing technologically advanced products for your company. At the beginning of each project, the project leader sits down with you and the other engineers and clearly specifies the roles and responsibilities of each team member. She also clearly specifies the type of product she wants you to engineer and the time frames involved. Finally, she makes sure that there is "buy-in" for the project, and gets agreement from everyone involved that they clearly understand the assignment and feel that they have the skills and talent to complete the assigned job. So far so good, right?

Unfortunately, as the project proceeds, you and your co-workers become more and more inefficient. The project bogs down, and the project leader has to step in to correct your team's errors and inefficiencies. Obviously, this is not an optimal situation. The project leader comes to you and asks for your advice on how to improve the performance of your team. You have some ideas, but you want the project leader to come to her own conclusions, and so you use the Einstein strategy.

You ask the project leader to create a metaphor for how she views her role in optimizing the performance of your team. Enlightened manager that she is, she agrees to try the exercise. Interestingly, she depicts herself as a source of light, much like a lighthouse. She sees a bright reddish light emanating from her head to the team members, whom she imagines to be like ships floating in the ocean. While the ships are nearby, her light is able to guide them to their destination and enable them to avoid the rocks near the shoreline. But as the ships get further away, they lose sight of the guiding light and begin to flounder at sea.

To maximize the potential value of this exercise, you ask the project leader to list the assumptions inherent in her constructed metaphor. Upon further analysis, she realizes that her metaphor contains two important assumptions: first, that the light was sufficient for navigation (it wasn't; a lighthouse helps the ship stay off the rocks, not necessarily navigate successfully—especially in rough waters), and second, that ships do not have their own sources of light (they might) and are always sailing in the dark.

Could the team leader create a new metaphor that eliminated, in some way, the two previous assumptions? In her second metaphorical construction, she still visualized herself as a lighthouse. But instead of sending out a bright red light for short periods of time, she saw herself emanating a soft but constant pinkish light. After a period of time, little pink and reddish lights would begin to flicker on board some of the ships, ultimately growing bright enough to cast light and provide guidance for their own ships and for other ships (that is, other team members) in the harbor as well.

Step-by-Step Instructions for Using the Einstein Strategy in a Group

1. The meeting leader describes a problem or goal to the group members.
2. Each member of the group (including the leader) draws a metaphoric picture to represent his or her understanding of the problem.
3. All group members share and explain their pictures.
4. The group as a whole discusses the assumptions inherent in each of the drawings.
5. Group members create new drawings that capture newly discovered points of view.
6. The group comes to closure by incorporating newly discovered insights into an overall plan for solving the original problem or achieving the original goal.

When the manager realized that the "ships" could have their own sources of light, she dramatically changed her management style. Her role switched from benevolent know-it-all to coach. For instance, rather than giving very precise instructions for a new project up front, she would start by giving only a general overview so that everyone involved could contribute, and feel—and in reality be—more a part of the process. And after the general overview, she also had all the team members do what "you" had recommended that she do, namely, construct their own metaphors to represent their feeling for the overall project and their specific contributions as they envisioned them.

The bottom line (and this example is based on a true story) was that the team performance experienced an immediate, dramatic, and measurable (quicker turnaround time, significantly fewer errors, etc.) change for the better. Of course, as one team member was heard to say, it never hurts to have an Einstein (or at least his way of thinking) on your team!

Experience has shown that the Einstein strategy of using constructed metaphors is particularly useful in solving seemingly unsolvable problems. Because of the strategy's inherent strength in questioning basic assumptions, it is especially powerful in helping to realign two seemingly diametrically opposed ideas or positions into win-win solutions. From the man who made it his life's work to demonstrate the fundamental connectedness and unity of the universe, why should we have expected any less?

■ 15 ━━━━━━━━━━━━━━━━━━

Meet the Inventors: Three Stories of Genius

For the past seven years, I have co-produced and hosted a cable show in Connecticut called "Meet the Inventors." I thought you might like to meet three of the inventors I interviewed on the show, and hear their inspiring (and instructive) stories of inventive genius.

Steven Chelminski: Nothing Is Impossible

Steven Chelminski's most successful invention is a device that can be towed behind a ship to help chart the terrain of the ocean floor. Essentially, the device is designed to repeatedly explode on demand by releasing highly pressurized air. When tripped, it creates an explosion whose sound and shock waves are powerful enough to travel to the bottom of the ocean, through many layers of ocean floor sediment, and back to sensitive recording devices aboard the mother ship. Using a sonarlike detection system, the mother ship can record how long it takes the sound to return to the ship, and thus is able to chart the ocean bottom. Geologists can then analyze these recordings for possible oil deposits based on the configurations of the ocean terrain.

This invention revolutionized the oil-exploration industry. Before Chelminski's invention, oil-exploration ships used dynamite to make their explorations, which was dangerous, expensive, and often unreliable. Even the most efficient explorer ships could explode only one dynamite charge per minute. With Chelminski's air-pressure device, inexpensive, safe, and controlled "explosions" could be made every eight to ten seconds. The result was more detailed, accurate, and reliable maps. For the consumer, it meant lower prices for oil and gas.

Steve has also invented, among other things, a simpler kind of rocket booster and a new pair of shoes.

Unfortunately, he never was able to make any money on the shoes. In a classic case of building a better mousetrap, but *not* having the world beat a path to your door, Steve found holes developing in the soles of his leather shoes and began looking for a pair of more reliable, longer-lasting shoes. Unfortunately, "synthetic shoes," while they lasted longer, didn't have the breathability, look, or comfort of leather. He wanted leather, but then again he didn't want leather. Could he somehow make the sole only partly out of leather?

He got the idea of putting small urethane plugs (about twenty) in the soles of his shoes. Urethane is a relatively inexpensive, highly wear-resistant substance. With the introduction of these urethane plugs in the soles, he found he could indeed have the best of both worlds: the comfort, breathability, and look of leather, combined with the durability of urethane. An added benefit was that the plugs acted much like the gripping studs on car snow tires and prevented him from slipping on the ice or snow.

Steve patented the idea and went looking for a licensee. Unfortunately, he was never able to license his invention because the last thing shoe manufacturers want is a shoe that *doesn't* wear out!

The lesson here: You don't necessarily want to bring an invention to the company that's the leader in its field. That company has the most to lose from a new invention, and therefore is often the most resistant to considering new ideas.

■ ■ ■

Steve is constantly on the lookout for new problems to solve. This is one of the mindsets common to successful inventors. Another is the sense that nothing is impossible. This next story illustrates, better than any I know, this "nothing is impossible" spirit of inventive thinking.

Steve's father was dying of cancer. The doctors had tried everything—operations, chemotherapy—but the tumor kept coming back. Steve wouldn't give up, though. If the doctors couldn't do any more, then it was up to him to *invent a cure for cancer.*

The idea Steve came up with was to neutralize the tumor by implanting very small silver or gold pellets surgically into it. When exposed to a continual flow of high-frequency radio waves, the pellets would heat up and burn away the cancerous growth without injuring the surrounding healthy tissue—an ingeniously simple idea.

Unfortunately, Steve never got to try the invention. His father deteriorated rapidly, and died soon after. But the doctors at Yale New Haven hospital did feel that Steve's idea could theoretically have worked. To this day I marvel at Steve's willingness to try to find a solution to seemingly unsolvable problems.

Incidentally, I recently spoke to an inventor from the former Soviet Union, who tells me that a very similar idea using ferromagnetic particles to burn away cancerous tumors has been successfully tested in one of their medical research institutes.

Calvin MacCracken: The Inventor as Detective

Calvin MacCracken has more than 100 inventions to his credit. He invented the hot dog roller cooker that you see at most ball games, the air heating and air conditioning units on astronauts' space suits, and a new way to tie shoes. MacCracken invented an easier way to tie shoelaces when he was a mere three years old. Apparently his mother knew at that moment that she had given birth to an inventor.

MacCracken figures that if 10 percent of his inventions are real moneymakers, he is doing well. To improve his odds, he does a lot of talking to the market to find out what it wants and to continually improve and refine his basic ideas. An essential prerequisite for doing this kind of market research is, of course, that MacCracken not be fearful of someone's stealing his ideas. MacCracken feels the benefits of research far outweigh the risk of anyone's stealing an idea. This is a point of view held almost universally among the successful inventors I know.

MacCracken is also a strong proponent of the mentoring system. When he was young, he had the invaluable opportunity of working with Thomas Edison's inventive son Theodore whom MacCracken credits with doing some of the most important pioneering work on computers.

■ ■ ■

MacCracken also had an influential mentor at General Electric, Anthony J. Nerad, when they worked together on the design of the jet engine during World War II. MacCracken tells a fascinating story about once being invited to Nerad's house for dinner. Just before sitting down to eat, they were listening to an Edward R. Murrow live report of a V-1 buzz bomb about to hit London. Nerad cranked up the radio so he could hear the sound of the buzz bomb better. Then he ran over to his piano and found a corresponding note to match the sound.

From this sound, Nerad was able to deduce correctly to the astonishment of the War Department's top scientists, the essential mechanisms and operating principles of the bomb! How? Nerad had studied the design of pipe organs and knew that creating a desired tone required a definite volume of airspace. Different tones had different space requirements. To make the sound that it did, therefore, the buzz bomb had to be of a certain size and shape. From this size and shape information, he could then deduce the essential design and mechanisms of the bomb. Nerad and MacCracken spent most of the night doing actual diagrams and schematics of the device. They were so excited, they never did eat dinner.

The next day, they arranged a meeting with top War Department officials to present their discovery. MacCracken credits this instance of innovative thinking as the deciding factor in the War Department's decision to give GE the contract to make gas turbines for jet engines.

As a mentor, then, Nerad taught MacCracken that one of the keys to inventive thinking is the ability, at times, to think like a detective, to be able to work backwards from effects and imagine their possible causes.

Another key is not to let "insufficient information" prevent you from taking the information you do have and imagining possible solutions. Essentially, you need to become comfortable with, and indeed search out, ambiguity, inconsistencies, and incompleteness in the world around you. The more you can find what's missing, the more you'll discover what's needed.

Howard Wexler: Inspiration Is Everywhere

Howard Wexler is best known as the inventor of Connect Four, a three-dimensional tic-tac-toe game. Howard has invented scores of toys and games with retail sales in the tens of millions of dollars. I want to tell you about the genesis of two of Howard's inventions: sock puppets and Crunch balls.

If genius is the ability to see something so obvious that it is invisible to everyone else, then the invention of Howard's line of sock puppets is truly an act of genius. As its name implies, a sock puppet is a child's sock that has a character painted or sewn onto the end of it. The child can insert his hand in it, and voila! a puppet to entertain himself and his parents. Howard got the idea when he saw his son playing pretend with a sock. Inspiration struck. Simple. Obvious. And yet, how many of us with children have seen ourselves, or our children, do exactly the same thing: put one hand in a sock and play pretend? Howard was able to capitalize on this lucrative new product idea because he has trained his mind to be constantly alert for new product ideas. It's a matter of mindset and attention.

Howard's Crunch ball is a good example of another kind of mindset: continually being on the lookout for those things that are irritating, then transforming this irritation into a successful invention.

How often have you received a package that is filled with those awful Styrofoam packing "shells" that go everywhere when you try to empty the box? This environmentally wasteful Styrofoam packing material became so irritating to Howard one day that he decided he just had to do something with it. Instead of throwing the shells away, he'd find a use for them. So Howard asked an important question: What kind of toy could he invent with this stuff? That simple question led to the invention of Crunch balls, a line of easy-to-catch indoor balls filled with Styrofoam packing shells!

With the right questions, you can find inspiration everywhere.

Section Four

The World's Best Creative Techniques

■ 16

Putting the Image Back Into Imagination: The Magazine Cut-and-Paste Exercise

The *American Heritage Dictionary of the English Language* defines *imagination* as "the process or power of forming a *mental image* of something that is not or has not been seen or experienced."

Considering the above definition, what if you were asked to create an *imaginative* definition of "imagination"? Could you do it?

While you're thinking about it, let me give you three of mine:

- *Imagination* is a grinning chimpanzee dressed in a regal-looking purple robe sitting on a Louis XIV antique chair staring at a lush green forest through an eighteenth-century pirate's telescope.
- *Imagination* is a twelve-year-old boy's wonder-filled, wide brown eyes reflecting back to me images of the pulsating lightning bugs he's just released from his cupped hands.
- *Imagination* is two one-inch robots walking through a three-dimensional stainless steel maze trying to find a pocket watch in the center of the maze that Einstein (chin in hand, looking at the maze from above) has left there.

One of the most powerful all-purpose creative techniques I know of is the magazine cut-and-paste exercise. I've used it for everything from training computer salespeople to be more creative in their sales presentations, to naming a new snack food, to creating more dynamic and memorable speeches, to, well, finding an imaginative definition for the word "imagination."

The magazine cut-and-paste exercise does indeed allow you to put the image back into imagination. What I particularly like about this technique is that you can generate literally an unlimited number of possible answers for so seemingly mundane and limited a task as defining the word "imagination." Also, as with the imagination (and unlike, say, in school), there are no right or wrong answers.

The unlimited and visually individualizing elements of this technique make it particularly useful for eliciting intuitions and ill-defined, unconscious feelings about a particular assignment, topic, problem, product, or service. How does your staff really feel about that new incentive program? What would your best customers most want in a new product? What is your company's mission, and how does it translate into a vision for the future? Because the magazine cut-and-paste technique accesses the right brain, your more visual, feeling part of the brain, it truly does give you an entirely different way of *looking* at a problem.

The ability to make the abstract visually concrete (as in the above definitions of imagination) is a hallmark of many of history's greatest scientific geniuses. Research suggests that Einstein, Edison, da Vinci, electrical inventor Nikola Tesla, and physicists James Clerk Maxwell and Michael Faraday, for instance, all had early learning disabilities with a decided preference for *visual modes of processing* their worlds.[1] Not surprisingly, it was this ability to visualize that these scientists felt was most often responsible for their creative breakthroughs.

Visual Selling

A short time ago, an electronic controls and robotics company in the Midwest asked me to help "teach their salesmen to be more creative." Of the twenty or so creativity exercises I had the sales force try throughout the day, by far the most effective was the magazine cut-and-paste exercise. Here's how it worked:

- I passed out old magazines and scissors.

- I had each salesperson make a collage of the cutouts of all his or her favorite things: fast cars, beautiful men or women, sports, foods, etc.

- Each salesperson was then asked to assign a word to each of the pictures on the montage.

- The salesperson then had to transform the sales pitch into one large metaphorical word picture by completing the sentence, "Our product is a lot like a ____ (insert a word from the montage) because it ____ ." For instance, a salesperson might say, "Our product is a lot like a *filet mignon steak* because *we've trimmed all the fat from it."* At first, the salespeople found it very difficult to make analogies between their products and their "favorite things." But soon they were making some truly ingenious connections. Ultimately, they discovered new, often more compelling, ways of thinking about and selling their products.

Visual "Visioning"

Finding a workable "vision" for your company or department can be a daunting task. Ideally, the vision should be simple, short, emotionally compelling, easily internalized and remembered by staff members, aligned with short- and long-term company goals, and future- and goal-oriented. The marketing department of a $100 million computer consulting firm recently asked me to assist them in the generation of just such a departmental vision and mission statement.

The magazine cut-and-paste exercise was a tremendous asset in evolving the department's mission statement. Each employee was asked to create a montage of "images that capture the feeling of our mission." One manager pasted pictures of a variety of tools (a knife, a fork, a paintbrush) in the center of her montage. As she and the other staff members discussed the relevance of her tool metaphor, they came to realize that one of the primary missions of the marketing department was to develop and disseminate "tools" that would help make other departments become successful in accomplishing their missions.

Thanks to the magazine cut-and-paste exercise, the image of "tool makers" and "tool providers" helped marketing crystallize in a simple, clear, and memorable way its broader service role within the corporation.

Visual Speechmaking

One of the ways to build a memorable and powerful speech is to speak in what I call word pictures. (See page 130.) The magazine cut-and-paste exercise can help you do just that by turning abstract concepts into unforgettably vivid mental images. For example, let's say you've decided to run for President of the United States. You're running as an independent, and you have decided to focus your campaign around eliminating influence pedaling in Washington. Specifically, you want to curtail the role and power of lobbyists. You decide you need some word pictures to give your speeches some bite.

Here are a few ideas I came up with by using random images from magazines as idea starters:

- The ship of America's future has now shrunk to the size of a small raft, and the lobbyists are still handing out saws to all hands.
- The lobbyists will tell you Washington is like an elegant old pocket watch—if they're not there to wind it every day, everything will come to a standstill.
- If only lobbyists would stay in the lobby, instead of sneaking up to hotel rooms with our congressmen.
- Get on the lobby train and you may like the ride, but I guarantee you won't like the destination.
- Lobbyists have sucked so much of the life blood out of America, I think everyone in Washington should start carrying crucifixes, mirrors, and wooden stakes.
- Think of lobbyists as different brands of perfume. Individually, they each may smell pretty appealing, but as a group they stink.

Visual Design

The magazine cut-and-paste technique is also great for generating original design ideas. Eric Taub reports how Taurus used a variation of the magazine cut-and-paste exercise to help Ford create the unique, and at the time revolutionary, design of the Taurus:

■ ■ ■

Designers surrounded themselves with cutouts of other objects they admired, pictures they found in magazines, brochures, wherever they came across an illustration that represented a direction in which they wanted to expand. Photos of ski boots, cars, refrigerators, door handles, were all tacked around the work site. Stylists studied the trends to understand the competition, to know what direction design was progressing for all products.[2]

■ ■ ■

Visual Partying?

Believe it or not, I've even used the magazine cut-and-paste exercise to spice up a summer get-together. In a kind of "make a wish" party, I had the guests/friends do a magazine cut-and-paste collage of everything they'd wish for in their life if they could have anything.

To prepare for the event, I went to a local art supply store and got large sheets of white foam core. I thought some people might want to take their collages home and possibly even frame them.

As it turned out, I was right. After about an hour of cutting and pasting, we lined up all the "wish collages" in our living room for everyone to see. The effect was dramatic, powerful, even startling. These were genuine works of art. They were intriguing. They were beautiful. They were magnificent.

If you think about it, one of the reasons why the collages were so wonderful was because they literally had millions of dollars of production value in them. After all, these collages were made of images taken from ads and articles created by the world's greatest and best paid photographers and commercial artists.

Interestingly enough, two friends who were not particularly happy with their current lots in life (one was unhappy in his job; the other had just broken off a marriage engagement) had collages that although still quite beautiful, made them feel a little sad. Since they didn't feel good about themselves, they had trouble feeling good about their collages.

On the other hand, two of the partygoers were so excited about their collages that they had them framed.

Besides providing your guests with an unforgettable party experience, how else might you use the magazine cut-and-paste technique? I have one last suggestion: If you're looking to change careers, try using the magazine cut-and-paste exercise to help you identify those things you most love in life, and how they might form the basis for a new, creative career opportunity!

Notes

1. Thomas G. West, *In the Mind's Eye* (Buffalo, N.Y.: Prometheus Books, 1991).
2. Eric Taub, *Taurus, the Making of the Car That Saved Ford* (New York: Dutton Publishing, 1991), p. 108.

17

The Pringles® Paradox: Bill Gordon's Creativity Equation

After almost fifty years of research into the creative process, 200 patents, and an O'Henry Award for short story writing, William J. J. Gordon, the founder of Synectics, now president of SES Associates in Cambridge, Massachusetts, feels that he has finally produced a creativity system that reliably mirrors the analogy-forming process used by history's greatest inventors and thinkers—and now available to us all.

Somewhat surprisingly, the four-part "system" takes the form of a mathematical equation. It evolved, however, with anything but mathematical precision.

A Paradox at Tripoli Harbor

The first time Gordon experienced firsthand creative genius in action was during the North African campaign in World War II. He was part of a special Allied team assigned to clear Tripoli Harbor. The harbor was needed as a supply port for the invasion of Italy, and was therefore crucial. The Germans had scuttled a number of ships to block the harbor in such a way—with holes blocked by massive sheets of three-quarter-inch iron—that divers could not get in to patch the holes and float the ships.

A meeting was called to discuss what to do. As a naval officer was explaining the problem, Gordon noticed that an English colonel was listening with his eyes shut. After the naval officer finished, the English colonel, still with his eyes closed, spoke. (See the image streaming technique, page 92.) "Here is a ship built to specially travel great distances—and yet we can't move it a few feet. A most ingenious paradox.

"When my mother rakes out her walled-in garden in the middle of London," he continued, "she always ends up with a few high mounds of dirt. She can't throw the dirt over the wall . . . so she just rakes and rakes at those piles until the dirt gets spread around and disappears."[1]

The colonel opened his eyes, and those present realized that his mother had provided them with an ingenious solution. "We'll blast the ship to pieces with small cordite charges. Then we'll go down and rake the bloody mess until it's level."[2] Simple as it was, the idea worked beautifully.

From this first encounter with the hidden workings of the creative process, Gordon was inspired to evolve the present-day SES "equation for creativity." The equation consists of four steps:

---

1. Find the paradox inherent in your problem. 2. Find an analogue (analogy) that reflects the essence of the paradox. 3. Find the unique feature of the analogue. 4. Apply this unique feature to help you solve your problem.

---

1. *Find the paradox.* A problem by definition represents conflict. "And by looking for the paradox," says Gordon, "you'll force yourself to identify the core or essence of the problem you're trying to solve. Then you can find and apply a related analogue whose unique feature holds the promise, ultimately, of providing you with a truly breakthrough solution."[3]

An excellent example of the SES creativity technique in action is the development of a new wound healing bandage for the Israeli Air Force Medical Corps. The paradox inherent in conventional bandages is that although they protect the wound from outside germs, they also interfere with healing because they interrupt the body's "natural physiological flow."[4] As Gordon's team characterized the essence of the paradox, the bandage is a *wounding bandage.*

2. *Find an analogue (analogy) that reflects the essence of the paradox.* In this case, the team decided that the idea of fixing a cut light cord in a hurry was quite similar. "If you wind the tape carelessly you actually can put an insulating barrier between the wires you're trying to join. Thus your bandage sort of wounds the very thing you're fixing."[5]

3. *Find the unique feature of the analogue.* In the analogue of fixing a cut electric cord, "the essential activity was to close the circuit by twisting the wires back together to reestablish the flow of electricity."[6]

4. *Apply this unique feature to help you solve your problem.* When you twist wires back together, you reestablish the flow of electricity. The objective, then, of a newly designed bandage was to help you reestablish the flow of physiological current. How might you do this? The team designed a bandage containing magnesium, a nontoxic conductor of elec-

tricity, to increase the flow of the body's own electric current to stimulate healing.

This is what the wound healing problem looks like in the SES creativity equation:

$$\frac{\text{The bandage prevents the wound from healing}}{\text{Reestablish the flow of physiological current}} = \frac{\text{Fixing a cut electric cord Tape prevents current flow}}{\text{Twist the wires to reestablish electricity flow}^7}$$

Gordon and Poze have used this creativity equation to help people develop everything from the trash compactor to Pringles® potato chips. In the case of Pringles, it was a matter of designing a new product and package that would allow a potato chip to be manufactured at a large and efficient central plant and be transported long distances, without spoiling or breaking and without the need to fill the bag with more air than chips. In essence, it would be a compact chip that would not destruct. The paradox of compact destruction led to his analogue from nature, leaves.

"When you try to shove a load of dry leaves into one of those plastic bags, you have a hell of a time. You seem to be packing air just the way the potato chip manufacturers do."[8] But when the leaves are wet (the unique feature), they are soft and formable, and very easily packed. The reason: A wet leaf conforms to the shape of its neighbor with little room for air in between. By wetting and forming dried potato flour, the packaging problem was solved, and Pringles had its start.

■ ■ ■

Another intriguing example of the creativity equation was a communication problem at a large teaching hospital. It seems that when the hospital was small and everyone knew one another, informal, impromptu meetings took place frequently. To the hospital administrators' credit, they recognized that not only were these informal meetings and casual conversations that occurred so effortlessly good for hospital morale, but a lot of good ideas came from them. The problem was that the hospital had become a victim of its own success. With its growth came more and more employees, who knew fewer and fewer of the other employees. The camaraderie, informal meetings, and casual conversations (not to mention the good ideas) were on the decline.

As you might expect, the hospital tried a variety of ways to stimulate these casual, idea trading (and idea generating) meetings: luncheons, cocktail parties, lectures, special dinners, roundtables, etc. These meetings worked when they were held to solve specific problems, but they didn't foster that old spirit of camaraderie and cross-fertilization of ideas. The SES team analyzed the problem and decided that the inherent paradox of the hospital's situation was that unless the gatherings were *unorganized*, they wouldn't produce effective ideas.

They then looked to nature to find a suitable analogue (step 2). The analogue they came up with: herring gulls. Herring gulls are *unorganized* scavengers, but they are *effective* survivors.

What's the unique activity (step 3) associated with the herring gulls' scavenging? The gulls gather for an easy meal when fishermen throw unsalable fish back into the sea.

So then the equivalent (step 4) of this unique activity of herring gulls might be to have people come together at the hospital to eat *convenient* food at *reasonable* prices.

The new idea, then: Have the hospital *serve inexpensive gourmet food in the hospital cafeteria*. By subsidizing the cost of the gourmet food in the cafeteria, the hospital administrators could essentially "guarantee" that employees would gather there (much like the herring gulls drawn to the free fishermen's food) to meet informally, mingle casually, and exchange ideas.

Notes

1. W. J. J. Gordon and Tony Poze, *The New Art of the Possible, The Basic Course in Synectics* (Cambridge, Mass.: Porpoise Books, 1981, 1987), p. 24.
2. Ibid.
3. Personal conversation with William J. J. Gordon, 1990.
4. Gordon, *The New Art of the Possible,* p. 38.
5. Ibid., p. 39.
6. Ibid., p. 49.
7. Ibid., p. 49.
8. Ibid., p. 41.

■ 18

Welcome to Movies of the Mind: The Image-Streaming Technique

I was working with the D. H. White Company, a successful commercial real estate firm in Connecticut, trying to create a series of elevator ads. It occurred to us that advertising in elevators would be a good way to reach potential office space clients. Although not a large assignment, it still needed to be done well. Even a medium-size commercial real estate deal could mean $100,000 or more in commissions to my client.

I'll never forget this assignment, not so much because of the results, which were very good, but because I found myself trying to visualize a solution instead of reasoning one out. Normally with an advertising assignment, I spend a lot of time talking to myself, asking and then answering questions. On this assignment, though, for whatever reason, in a moment of reverie, I simply closed my eyes and looked for pictures on my mental screen that might provide an answer.

Somewhat to my surprise, I immediately saw an elevator panel with several of the floor buttons on it lit up. Below the elevator panel, I saw the "open doors," "close doors," and "emergency stop" buttons. Finally, I found myself looking at the inside of the entire elevator compartment, with the elevator doors in the process of opening up. To my surprise, from these simple, effortlessly imagined images, I created a series of five ads. One depicted an elevator crowded with cartoon characters and the headline, "Need More Space?" Another was a drawing of an elevator panel with several of the floor buttons lit up, just as I had seen it on my mental screen. The headline read, "Are You Visiting One of Our Clients?" Another showed only the first-floor button lit up, my client's name next to it, and the headline, "Number One, Please."

Because this "passive visualization" process was so simple, effortless, and often quite effective, I continued to use it for other creative assignments. But it wasn't until I met Win Wenger, president of the Institute for Visual Thinking in Gaithersburg, Maryland, and developer of the creative technique known as image streaming that I added a second critical element to the process: verbal description. By describing the images, out loud, as they arise in the mind's eye, you can practice a kind of synesthesia, or synthesizing of the senses. (Synesthesia occurs when you overlap two or more senses together; see Disney, page 161.)

By adding the vocal, descriptive element to the visualization process, you engage more parts of the brain at any single moment, and therefore, potentially, use more of the brain's power to solve a problem.

Pioneering research with the image-streaming technique has indicated not only that it can be a powerful problem-solving technique, but also that it has the potential to dramatically increase *IQ levels*. In one study, for instance, with physics students at Southwest State University in Marshall, Minnesota, their IQ levels, on average, increased twenty points after only twenty-five hours of image streaming.

Intrigued? If you'd like to try the technique, here's how:

- Ask yourself (or have a partner ask you) a question—any question.

- Do not try to answer the question directly. Instead, close your eyes, relax, and without consciously trying to answer the question, begin to describe the images as they appear in your mind's eye. Talk about these images in the present tense ("I'm seeing . . .") and record them on a tape recorder or have a partner record them. Do this for a few minutes initially, thirty minutes or more once you get used to the technique.

- Study these images for their metaphorical value. What could that falling bridge you saw mean? How could a purple cactus in some way symbolize a solution to your problem? What does that William Tell-type crossbow have to do with your business anyway?

At first, like a dream, you may find these images, if not unnerving, then certainly a little weird. I encourage you to try and withhold judgment, and look for underlying meanings in these images, no matter how silly they seem. I have used this technique for everything from writing a more powerful, memorable, and "word-picture"-filled speech, to naming a new product, to generating new packaged-goods inventions, to even solving management and personnel problems.

Let me give you a real-world example from packaged-goods manufacturing. When I was asked to give a speech on business creativity to an MBA class on innovation at the University of Connecticut, I included several of my favorite creative techniques and a demonstration of how to use them to solve real-world problems. When it came time for a demonstration of image streaming, I asked the audience for a problem to work on, and a production expert from Clairol got up.

"We've been having some breakage on some of our hair conditioning bottles," he said. "If we don't maintain the bottle filling at a perfectly constant rate, sometimes there will be spaces between the bottles. When they go down the fill shoots, they don't have another bottle to cushion their fall, and so the bottle will crack or break." That was the problem. Pretty straightforward.

I closed my eyes and began image streaming. "I am seeing the inside of a throat. It's kind of red inside. Mucus is moving down the throat. I am now seeing the mucus being pushed along by the little hairlike projections on the throat, the cilia. They're like a wave of grain blowing in the wind, or even seaweed under the ocean flowing back and forth, ebbing and flowing with the current."

These were interesting images, were they not, to have "just appear" in my mind? Frankly, I'm always as amazed as the audience is when I see what comes out of this exercise.

Next came the analysis process. I threw it back to the MBA students. Could the images I just described in any way help us solve our manufacturing problem? How about you? Do you have any ideas?

We solved the problem without a great deal of effort: Add a series of thin plastic cilialike fingers in the fill shoots to slow the bottles when they didn't have other bottles to cushion their fall. Simple, and not particularly profound—but not bad either for literally 30 seconds of problem-solving time.

■　■　■

I have seen other problems solved just as quickly using the image-streaming technique. For example, in a workshop I did for a group of both established and aspiring entrepreneurs at the Entrepreneurial Center at Manhattanville College in New York, a businesswoman told me that she created a logo for her business (something she had been trying to do unsuccessfully for more than three months) in less than the two minutes I allowed for the demonstration of the technique. In another workshop, another businesswoman got "the big idea" for her company brochure (a children's travel service) in less than a minute of image-streaming time.

What I find most intriguing about this technique is that although we continually have pictures running through our minds, most of us choose not to pay attention to them. Much like dreams that never get analyzed (and yet potentially hold the key to resolving all manner of personal and professional problems), these images that are continually streaming through our minds hold untold problem-solving and creative riches. All we have to do is start paying attention to them. And, of course, learn to speak their language: the language of visual metaphor.

■ 19

Granola Sunny Side Up? Using Grids of Possibilities

"Aren't you the guy with the blocks?" this stranger on the street asked me.

Yes, as it turned out, I was the guy with the blocks. The night before I had been interviewed on a Connecticut TV talk show, and had brought with me three children's blocks to demonstrate a creative technique known as morphological analysis, or the matrix (or matrices) method. Or you might just call it, as I do, grids of possibilities.

Let me give you a real-world case history of the grids of possibilities technique in action before we discuss how and where you might consider using it.

Inventor and new product consultant Stan Mason knew that his secretary wished she could exert more will power when dieting. But every morning, when she picked up her coffee at the local doughnut place, she couldn't resist also having one of those delicious jelly doughnuts. This got Stan to thinking. Could he invent a more nutritious—and less fattening—on-the-go breakfast treat?

This simple question ultimately led to the invention of the granola bar. What's interesting is that by using the grids of possibilities technique to "explore all their options," as Mason put it, he and a team of marketing people and food engineers at Nestlé ultimately developed a product (and a market) quite different from the one they had originally intended.

By constructing grids of possibilities like the ones in Figure 19-1 the concept of a granola bar (originally conceived of as a nutritious, on-the-go breakfast food) was expanded to include, as Mason puts it, a "tasty lunch or after-lunch snack for children and young adults," which today is its primary market niche.

By considering each box in each grid, the developers got ideas for what kinds of ingredients to include in which products for which people and what time of day. In the breakfast boxes, for example, products were developed, and ultimately test-marketed, that included such seemingly exotic ingredients as bacon bits, orange peels, Rice Krispies, and even dried eggs. Fat-free nuts, including pistachios and almonds, were incor-

Figure 1. Abridged versions of two of the actual grids used to help develop the granola bar concept.

Where

	At home	At the office	Traveling	Entertaining	Eating out	Vending machines
Breakfast						
Mid-morning snack						
Brunch						
Lunch						
When Afternoon snack						
Tea time						
Dinner						
Nighttime snack						
Before-bed snack						
Anytime snack						

Who

	College	Blue-collar	White-collar	Elementary school	High school	Secretaries
Breakfast						
Mid-morning snack						
Brunch						
Lunch						
When Afternoon snack						
Tea time						
Dinner						
Nighttime snack						
Before-bed snack						
Anytime snack						

porated into lunch, afternoon, and party-time versions; and sweeter versions, with chocolate chips and higher percentages of sugar, were designed for afternoon and evening treats for children.

As inventor Mason says of the grid approach to new product development, "These grids force you to one of the true secrets of inventing: namely, to carry on a dialogue with yourself, and ask yourself questions you might not always think to ask."

In another grid (not pictured), other "who's" included a variety of sporting and exercise groups and activities. One of these groups, "mountain climbers," gave the development team the idea of incorporating a mountain peak in the package design as a way of implying a high-energy snack.

How might you use a grid to help you ask questions you may not be asking, solve problems you may not be solving, and generate a host of alternative ideas? Grids can be used for a variety of creative problem-solving assignments, from new product naming and development to creating advertising concepts/target markets, and even grouping ideas generated in a brainstorming session for future action plans. All you need are two (or more) sets of variables or parameters for the x and y axes.

New Product Grids of Possibilities

Take, for instance, the new product consulting work I once did for a large cheese company. One of the ideas we were considering was a new line of soft cheese spreads to make quicker and tastier grilled cheese sandwiches. Preliminary focus groups with consumers indicated that because the cheese was spreadable, they did think the "Cheese Grills" would cook up faster, but that they were not necessarily convinced that spreadable cheese would be tastier. And so the idea of adding other ingredients to the basic cheese spreads became an attractive alternative. For our grid of possibility, we listed the kinds of cheese across the top (cheddar, Swiss, Muenster) and the other ingredients down the side (bacon bits, tomato paste, olives, relish). Some interesting combinations emerged, such as Muenster Bacon, Olive Swiss, and Cheddar Relish.

Naming Grids of Possibilities

Or consider a naming assignment we did for a new cheese Frito, where we listed all the things that our target market (males aged 18 to 25) purported to like (guns, fishing, baseball, pickup trucks, and girls) on one axis and the special qualities or descriptors of what made our snack different (better taste, more "powerful" cheese flavor, longer-lasting flavor) on the other axis, and looked for connections or associations between the two. Great White Cheddar, Cheddar Blasts, Cheddar Bangs, and Non-Stop Nachos were among the names generated from this exercise. And the winner? The product was launched nationally as Non-Stop Nachos. By the way, we also used the magazine cut-and-paste exercise in this assignment as a way to generate the categories of things males aged 18 to 25 liked and some feelings about what made this new cheese Frito different. (See page 83.)

Grids of Possibilities in the Third Dimension

If you were wondering what "the guy with the children's blocks" has to do with all this, it was my way of demonstrating to a TV audience how grids of possibilities could be used to generate new game or toy ideas.

Here's what I did. I got three large children's blocks and glued a different word to each of the six faces on the blocks. Block number one had simple elements or features of a game or toy, block number two had actual toys, and block number three had leisure-time activities. Here are the examples:

Block 1	Block 2	Block 3
1. Velcro	yo-yo	fishing
2. magnets	squirt gun	gambling
3. string	Frisbee	tennis
4. pictures	ball	traveling
5. marbles	jump rope	bowling
6. mirrors	doll	painting

Then I simply rolled the blocks and started combining the words that came up to see what inventions they suggested. See if the following combinations suggest any ideas to you, as they did for me.

- Squirt gun, painting, marbles
- String, Frisbee, bowling
- Mirrors, jump rope, painting
- Doll, Velcro, fishing
- Yo-yo, marbles, gambling

This made for a fun, powerfully visual, and apparently memorable way to expose the audience to the grids of possibilities technique.

You might consider adapting this grids of possibilities block exercise to one of your problem-solving sessions. What better way to start building new ideas than with building blocks?

20

Who Am I, Anyway? The Role-Playing Technique

Have you ever tried to come up with an idea to generate excitement at a company's trade show booth? It's not easy. Several years ago Hipp Waters, a Connecticut personnel firm, asked me to do just that. It could be a contest, a demonstration, a singing magician, whatever. The one requirement was that the idea somehow relate to the personnel industry.

I began the assignment by fantasizing. What would make me want to stop by a personnel firm's booth—especially since I was neither looking for work nor hiring? Let's see. If I were guaranteed to meet a future client, I'd certainly stop by. If Neil Simon were there, I'd stop and ask him how to create memorable characters. If a reporter for *The Wall Street Journal* were there looking to do a feature story on someone at the trade show, I'd also stop by. If I could ask the head of the CIA a question and be guaranteed a truthful answer, I'd certainly stop.

All this fantasizing was fun—so much so that it got me to thinking. Why not let the trade show attendees fantasize right along with me and think about what their *fantasy job* might be? Astronaut, rock star, forest ranger, spy—what would they be doing if they could do anything? We'd offer prizes to everyone who entered our survey/contest, and even send them a summary of the results (in exchange for their business cards, of course). Hipp Waters could also do follow-up stories with the media reporting the results of their "fantasy job" poll.

In all, 596 people entered the survey/contest. Respondents were able to choose one of twenty-eight fantasy occupations, ranging from actor to zoo keeper. The results were fascinating. Among these ostensibly conservative businesspeople, the number one fantasy job was *secret agent!* Other top choices, in order of preference, included:

2. Actor
3. U.S. Senator
4. Rock star

5. Artist
6. Astronaut
7. Safari guide
8. Comedian
9. Inventor
10. Professional athlete
11. Novelist
12. Chief

The tremendous interest in our trade show promotion, coupled with the successful follow-up media coverage, confirmed something I suspected all along: People like to fantasize about having what other people have and doing what other people do. It can be a powerful human motivator. It can be a lot of fun. It can also be the source of breakthrough ideas.

Role-Playing My Mother-in-Law

In the creativity literature, adopting the role or persona of another person, living or dead, is known as the role-playing technique. In role playing, you simply pretend that you are someone else. Then you ask this "person" inside you for ideas. It is amazing, but the human mind really can imagine how someone else might think about, or even solve, a problem that "we" can't solve. We can hear what "they" have to say about it, and be the beneficiary of their advice. It's as if their voices live inside us, just waiting to be asked what they think. It's a simple, profound, and remarkably powerful technique, one that you can use either alone or with groups.

Often, when I use the technique in ideation sessions, I'll pass out identity cards with a picture and short biography of the role each person is to adopt. Some of my identity cards include photographers Mathew Brady and Ansel Adams, Florence Nightingale, Frank Lloyd Wright, Abraham Lincoln, Ben Franklin, Walt Disney, Will Rogers, Thomas Edison, Dr. Seuss (Theodor Geisel), and Madame Tussaud (of wax museum fame). Then I'll simply go around the room, have everyone introduce "themselves," and ask for their input on the problem. (*Note:* It's the facilitator's responsibility to make sure that everyone stays in character.)

To role-play alone, I'd recommend having your adopted persona write "his or her" responses down. Or you might try using the creativity computer program Idea Generator Plus, which has a role-playing feature as one of its idea generating techniques. When I wrote a review of the Idea Generator Plus for *Lotus* Magazine, I discovered in an interview with Randy Fields, CEO of Mrs. Fields cookies, that he will occasionally hold a meeting with his senior managers *without any of them being present*. He simply enters their names into the program, then imagines the responses and recommendations each manager will give to his questions.

Are you skeptical? You'd be surprised. Once you get the hang of it, it's quite easy to do. I know because I used the role-playing feature of Idea Generator Plus to help me invent a new game.

In my case, I had spent several months creating a prototype of an adult entertainment game that turned anyone and everyone into an instant inventor. When I went to play-test the game, however, it didn't really work. Players weren't having nearly as much fun as I'd hoped they would. And so I tried Idea Generator Plus in the hope that it could help me redesign the game. I held an imaginary brainstorming session that included, among other invited guests, my mother-in-law. It was "her" question, "Is there some way to make the game simpler?" that led me to eureka! With this simple imagined, but also very real, question from "her," I suddenly knew how to redesign the game to make it work. And work it did. Ultimately, I licensed the invention to a major game company.

Role Playing for the Navy

Often, when I run a brainstorming session, I'll invite outside creative consultants to be part of the session. I got to know a kind of modern-day Renaissance man named Ted Cheney in just such a way when we were brainstorming new amusement rides and equipment for a large industrial equipment manufacturer.

Ted has written several books, both nonfiction and fiction, started his own natural resources exploration company, worked for several new product development firms, and even traveled with Admiral Byrd to the South Pole. He now teaches Writing at Fairfield University in Connecticut.

During one of the breaks, Ted and I got to talking about the new product development work he had done some years back as a consultant to the U.S. Navy. His team was brainstorming survival techniques for downed Navy fliers and adrift Navy seamen. One of the creative techniques the group used to attack the problem was role playing. One of the participants was asked to pretend that he was Davy Jones, living in his "locker" several thousand feet below the ocean's surface. How might Davy Jones help the stranded Navy man? "Davy" got the idea that if he could continually blow bubbles up to the surface, the bubbles would form a kind of safe, air-cushioned bubble barrier to protect the Navy man both from prolonged contact with salt water and from sharks. An intriguing idea, isn't it? Does it suggest any practical new inventions?

You might be surprised that this exercise didn't lead to a new air-cushioned survival suit at all, but to a new antisubmarine defense system. The group got to thinking about underwater bubbles, and it occurred to one of the scientists that air bubbles might be used to mask sounds under the water. The idea: Have a ship surround itself with millions of tiny air bubbles to mask the sound signatures of its engines and propellers. The group became very excited about the idea and passed it on to Naval Headquarters. What ever happened to it? The group never heard. Ted suspects that it was immediately classified so top secret that even its creators could not be told of its existence.

By the way, did you read Tom Clancy's book *Red Storm Rising*? If you do, you'll find the following passage:

■ ■ ■

> Prairie/Masker was a system for defeating submarine sonars. Two metallic bands surrounded the frigate's hull, fore and aft of the engine spaces. This was Masker. It took compressed air and bled it into the water around the ship in the form of millions of tiny bubbles. The Prairie part of the system did the same with the propeller blades. The air bubbles created a semipermeable barrier that tended to trap sounds made by the ship, letting only a fraction of her propulsion noise escape— which made the ship extremely difficult to detect.[1]

■ ■ ■

The Superhero Technique

An intriguing variation of the role-playing technique is the superhero technique, invented by Maple Shade, New Jersey, creativity consultant, author, and friend Steve Grossman. The superhero technique also involves role playing, but with an important difference from conventional "acting-out" exercises. Because participants are asked to adopt the persona of an *imaginary* character, they are often much freer, and therefore more likely to get into character, than if they were pretending to be a real-life person like Walt Disney or Thomas Edison. As one previously up-tight participant put it, "Sometimes you have to put on a mask to take your mask off." There is nothing quite like the prospect of wielding super-human powers to help free one's imagination!

The way it's played is to assign one person the role of client. (He'll be the only one, with the exception of the professional facilitator, who doesn't get to be a superhero.) The other members of the group then select a superhero they want to be from a list of ten or more choices. The superheros can be "known" heros (Spiderman, Captain America, Cat

Woman, The Invisible Man, The Incredible Hulk, Batman, Superman, etc.), or they can be created by the participant. Everyone is then given one-half hour to create a costume out of everyday objects that might be found inside (or outside) the brainstorming room. When everyone has made a costume and reassembled in the room, the designated client begins asking each superhero for ideas to solve the problem. Incredibly, after a very few minutes, each brainstormer really does begin to adopt the persona of his or her chosen superhero.

Let's look at a real-world example. The client's problem was this: How could he keep his marketing vice-president from monopolizing, and essentially disrupting, the national sales meeting, as he had done the previous year?

Ultimately, it was E-Man who provided the answer (E-Man, in case you didn't know, has infinite energy because he is made of pure energy. He also sleeps in a toaster.) E-Man decided to "melt the marketing vice-president's lips together." Interestingly, when the group further brainstormed how to make this seemingly absurd idea a reality, they got the idea of making the marketing vice-president chair of the meeting. By being made responsible for seeing that other people were heard, the marketing vice-president, at least metaphorically, would have his own lips "melted together."

In another example, U.S. Army avionics engineer Ray Clark was asked to help the manager of a regional Social Security office improve intradepartmental communication. Specifically, there was a problem with interoffice memos: They often got lost or were never read. Spiderman came to the rescue and "threw his spider net" around every employee in the office. This led to the idea for a computerized local area network to instantly distribute memos while ensuring they didn't get lost.

Note

1. Tom Clancy, *Red Storm Rising* (New York: Berkeley Publishing, 1987), p. 182.

■ 21 ▬▬▬▬▬▬▬▬▬▬▬▬▬▬▬▬▬▬

Naming Pepsi: The Briefing Document

A good way to make sure your brainstorming session hits the ground running is to prepare a briefing document. As its name implies, a briefing document is a written report that briefs all the session participants, generally a week or so in advance of the actual session, about the problem(s) the group is trying to solve.

The briefing document should also include creative exercises specific to the problem that encourage the participants to start getting ideas. For example, suppose you wanted to brainstorm more effective ways to communicate with your customers. Your briefing document might include exercises that forced group members to think about the nature of communication: What would be the advantages of using smoke signals rather than a telephone? If all your employees were telepathic, how might this help business? What if they couldn't hear, or see, or speak?

Or suppose you wanted to invent a line of new kitchen implements. Your briefing document might include a list of kitchen activities: e.g., dicing, slicing, shredding, boiling; identify the problems associated with these activities, e.g., cut or burnt fingers; and ask the participants for preliminary new product ideas.

In one session I facilitated to create new product ideas for a maker of polyurethane foam, we included in our briefing document an imaginary tour of the kitchen, the dining room, the bedroom, the living room, the garage, a tool shop, and a gardener's shed. By helping the participants to visualize these rooms and locations, and by providing lists of specific objects or things they might see when they got there, we helped them imagine possible new product ideas and uses for the urethane foam. One participant said the briefing document helped him to "see an ugly, brown television cord plugged into a living room wall. It made me wonder if we could create a line of designer polyurethane covers for electric cords to make them look prettier and go with the room better. Maybe they could be insulated to help prevent fires as well."

Beyond the sheer number of good (and sometimes great) ideas that your participants will bring to the session, the briefing document will help prime their subconscious minds so that when they attend the actual session, they'll be more likely to contribute a truly great idea.

The briefing document has two major sections: the introduction and the creative exercises.

Let's look at the introduction first. This should include both a brief description of the background and goal of the assignment and a general discussion of how the creative process works (why quantity of ideas leads to quality, why it's important not to be overly judgmental of one's responses, and why it's important to have fun in a session). Often I will include creative case histories to highlight these points. (For example, see the "how-to-manufacture nylon" anecdote on the value of creative horseplay, page 162.)

In the introduction, I also like to give the participants a reason for them to take the time to fill out the briefing document. Specifically, I tell participants that by filling it in beforehand, they'll be inviting their subconscious minds to be part of the process. Giving their conscious minds some specific creative exercises in advance of the session will allow their *subconscious* minds to become sufficiently primed for their creative problem-solving role in the actual session.

Next, I'll use the introduction to take some of the mystery, and possibly the fear, out of the session for those people who have never been in a formal brainstorming session before. For instance, I might mention that each member has been invited to the session because of his or her special knowledge of a particular subject, and that it will be up to the facilitator to see that everyone feels comfortable with his or her respective contribution.

I'll also use the introduction to create a level of mental comfort for the sometimes outlandish creative exercises. Here's an excerpt from an actual briefing document:

■ ■ ■

Some of the following exercises may seem a little strange. Don't worry about that. There is a method to the madness. You'll understand when you get into the session. For now, have fun and enjoy these short creative exercises.

■ ■ ■

The final element of the introduction is a time statement: "Time to complete: less than 1 hour."

Section two is the creative exercises themselves. I thought you might like to see six of the actual exercises I created for a Pepsi naming assignment. In addition to the exercises themselves, I'm including my rationale for each exercise in the briefing document.

Naming a New Soft Drink for Pepsi

> Oh, what's in a name?
> Is it all just a game?
> Would a rose smell as sweet,
> If its name were NutraSweet?"

Pepsi International asked me to help name a new sugarless soft drink that is now being marketed around the world. As part of the assignment, I facilitated an all-day naming/brainstorming session with top Pepsi executives. Among those present were people from marketing, consumer research, and product development. We also invited several creative outsiders (a freelance artist and an aspiring screenwriter, to name two) to attend the session. It was a very successful session. In all, we generated more than 550 names, including the winner.

Let's look at each of the briefing document exercises.

■ ■ ■

Exercise 1: Find an object that represents or symbolizes to you what this naming session is all about. Please draw the object, and also bring it to the session. Why do you think it represents or is a symbol for this naming assignment?

Explanation: One of the keys to right-brain thinking is the ability to find metaphors or symbols for the thing you're trying to explain or understand. This exercise is a simple, yet powerful way to promote this kind of analogical thinking. Having the participants draw the object forces them to spend more time on and give more attention to the object's "analogical potential" than they might normally. Drawing often helps people discover some facet or analogical feature that they would have missed with only a cursory review.

Exercise 2: What did you dream of being as a kid? An astronaut? A fireman? A nurse? A cowboy? List one or more of your childhood dreams below.

Explanation: There are two reasons for including this exercise. First, it gets people remembering their childhood state of mind, where anything was possible. This kind of fantastical, wish-for-anything, anything-can-happen mindset is obviously very useful in a brainstorming session. The second reason is to prepare the group for excursions (mental trips to other worlds) the day of the session. Often when a group's energy is low, I'll take the group on an excursion by suggesting we forget the problem for a minute and pretend, say, that it's early morning in the south of France.

We're flying in a balloon, and John over here has just uncorked a bottle of champagne. I ask the participants what they're thinking, feeling, and seeing. When I bring the group back, we check to see if what we saw, heard, or felt "while we were away" gave us any ideas for solving the problem. By having each participant describe what he or she dreamed of, I can create a list of possible places for the excursion that I know will be appealing to members of the group: we'll go to the Old West for the aspiring cowboy, a hospital for the nurse, and outer space for the astronaut.

Exercise 3: Because of your enthusiasm, the group has appointed you head cheerleader for this naming project. Imagine now that it is the end of the naming session. You have been successful in leading—and inspiring—us to create the winning name. The group has asked you to lead a cheer and spell out the winning name by *forming the letters with your body!* For some reason, though, you can't remember what the winning name is. You go ahead anyway and form some of the letters that might have been in the name.

Note: Please do not "think" about this exercise. Just start forming letters and see what you get. They don't have to be in any particular order.

Explanation: This is probably the strangest of all the exercises, but it has an important brainstorming function. Research has shown that people learn best in different ways. Most of us prefer one of three processing modes: visual, auditory, or kinesthetic (body oriented/feeling). This exercise champions the kinesthetic mode. By involving our bodies and our sense of touch and feel in the brainstorming process, we can often arrive at insights into a problem we simply could get no other way. Think about the phrase "gut feel."

Often, the result of this exercise is that someone will come to the session saying something like, "I'm not sure why, but I kept thinking the winning name will begin with the letter *T.*"

Exercise 4: List five names of products or services that you think are great. What specifically do you like about each?

Explanation: One of the most valuable naming exercises I know of is to analyze successful names for their inherent principles of genius, then try to apply these principles to other naming problems. When participants have analyzed great names like Lean Cuisine, Dry Idea, Lexus, SlimFast, and Salon Selectives for their principles of genius, it makes it that much easier for them to apply these principles to our assignment.

Exercise 5: Write a four-line nonsense poem about this naming exercise. And yes, it has to rhyme!

Explanation: Singing invokes a different part of the brain than speaking. This "poetic exercise" is designed to begin to sensitize the participants to the rhythms and cadences of words. I ask participants to create a *nonsense* poem for two reasons. First, I don't want them to freeze up on this exercise and become overly analytical, or to try to create "Ode on a Grecian Urn" or some such thing. Second, nonsense poems can provide a wonderful bit of relief and fun if and when I ask the participants to read their poems at the actual session. The NutraSweet poem above is one that came out of the Pepsi session.

Exercise 6: You are invited to a word party. To play, simply combine one of the word roots on the left side with one of the beverage-specific words on the right. Please coin five new words.

		The right side	
		included	
The left side		*beverage-*	
included such		*specific words*	
word roots as:		*like:*	
dec	hemi	ade	ola
aero	oid	pop	sip
quas	ix	soda	nutr
tri	digi	vim	swig
equ	plus	x-tra	gulp
max	visi	flow	drink
ast	dyna	squirt	cool
nutra	tex	pep	wet

Explanation: Dynapop. Nutragulp. Vimplus. You get the idea. The object here is to get people beyond the limitations of known words, exploring new possibilities and combinations. The exercise helps participants open up their minds to other possibilities, and sometimes triggers a known (but surprising) word or word pairing that gives us "the answer."

By the way, if you're curious, the winning name was Pepsi Max.

22

Jogging Your Imagination: The Wishing-Diamonds Technique

You've decided to look for a new job. Instead of approaching the job hunt in a conventional way, however, you decide to first try a no-holds-barred, nothing is impossible exercise in wishing to imagine what the perfect job-hunting experience might be like. See if some of your wishes don't agree with mine:

- I wish I could interview with the CEOs and presidents, not the personnel directors, of all the top companies I'd like to work for.
- I wish I could tell the CEOs and presidents exactly the day and time that I'd like to meet with them, and they would agree to see me at my convenience.
- I wish they'd treat me like a VIP of sorts, and give me a personal tour of their company and introduce me to their best people.
- Since I want to get a job as soon as possible, I wish I could meet with all these CEOs and presidents very quickly—maybe see up to twelve CEOs in one day, thirty-six in three days.
- From these thirty-six interviews, I'd like to have three or four job offers so that I could pick and choose the company I'd like to work for.
- And finally, since I don't enjoy getting dressed up, I'd like to wear comfortable clothes for all my job interviews.

How does this sound? Pretty ridiculous, right? Except that when I went job hunting, every single one of these wishes actually came true.

When I got out of school and first began looking for work in advertising, I got tired of the rejections pretty quickly, and decided there simply had to be a better way. I began to imagine how I might turn something that had become very unpleasant and psychologically debilitating into something self-affirming and fun.

My fantasies ultimately led me to create a publicity stunt called jogging for jobs, in which I and other job hopefuls (whom I had found by placing an ad in *The New York Times*) dropped off our résumés at New York City's top thirty-six advertising agencies over a three-day period. Because of the media attention, including two lead write-ups in the advertising column of *The New York Times* and coverage by the AP wire service and several New York radio and television stations, the advertising agencies rolled out the red carpet. At most agencies, either the CEO or the president greeted us. Several agencies even threw us parties. And since we were jogging, we were able to wear sweat pants and running shoes for our "interviews." And most of us (including myself) got jobs out of it.

I hope this story demonstrates, in part, the power of wishing as a creative technique. Wishing is the most effective way I know of to start fresh on any given problem. Wishing allows you to challenge your basic assumptions—assumptions that many times you may not even have known you were making—and get entirely new and original (not to mention fun) points of view. When for the longest time you may have felt like a beggar asking for a few crumbs of creative inspiration, wishing will turn you into a master baker of the most exciting (and delicious) creations imaginable.

Starting to Wish

How do you start using the wishing technique? Pretend that you can have anything you want, whenever and wherever you want it. There are absolutely no limitations. If you like, imagine that a genie has just appeared and is ready to grant you (at least) those wishes. Couldn't be easier, right?

You'd be surprised how hard it is for most people to allow themselves to even try this exercise, much less entertain the the possibility that there might be some value in it. We all have been so brainwashed into "being realistic" about life that we cannot allow ourselves, even in a purely theoretical exercise, to "make a wish." Why, after all, should we waste our valuable time thinking about things that are impossible anyway?

The paradox is that it's only by first considering the impossible that we can know the outer limits of what is possible, and therefore the potentially most exciting ideas.

How can you harness the power of wishing to generate new and better ideas within your company? In the worlds of creativity and innovation consulting, a process has evolved that provides a step-by-step approach for using the wishing technique successfully. Synectics principal Jeff Mauzy has included the process in his MindLink creativity computer program. A variation of the same process is used by one of my early brainstorming faciliting coaches, Dr. Christopher W. Miller, and his Lancaster, Pennsylvania, company Innovation Focus. Unable to leave well enough alone, I have adapted and modified the principles of the basic process into a somewhat simpler, and I think more memorable, technique that I call "wishing diamonds."

As you can see in the diagram in Figure 2, there are essentially three major sections, or diamonds, in the wishing-diamonds technique. In the top half of diamond one, you start by wishing for anything and everything. (In creativity terms, this is called *divergent thinking* and is represented by the lines making up the top half of the diamond going out, or diverging.) After generating the wishes (as many as you think appropriate), select one of the wishes on which you would like to do some further work. (In creativity terms, this process of selecting an idea is called *convergent thinking* and is represented by the lines making up the bottom half of the diamond coming back together, or converging.)

■ ■ ■

Now you are ready to enter diamond two. The object here is to brainstorm how to make the selected wish from diamond one, no matter how far our or seemingly absurd, a reality. Since it is often impossible to do this, brainstorm how to *approximate* the wish by achieving something similar to the desired effect. (This is where the "could we," "how about," and "what if" questions, again a divergent phase of the process, come in.) For example, suppose that in diamond one I had wished that I could travel from New York to Los Angeles instantaneously. Obviously this is not yet possible. But we can try to approximate this idea. How about doing a video teleconference? It is certainly one alternative to instantaneous travel. Or what if we gave you a coma-inducing drug in New York and an antidote to the drug in Los Angeles? For all intents and purposes, your perception would be that you had traveled from New York to Los Angeles instantaneously.

In the bottom half of diamond two, you select (the lines are once again converging) the one approximation (videoconferencing or coma) that you'd like to explore further.

■ ■ ■

Now you're ready to enter diamond three. Here you generate (diverge) a list of pluses and minuses (or challenges) to the implementation of the idea you selected from diamond two. (The minuses, or challenges, can be also phrased as "how to . . ." followed by ideas for overcoming the

Figure 2. Wishing diamonds.

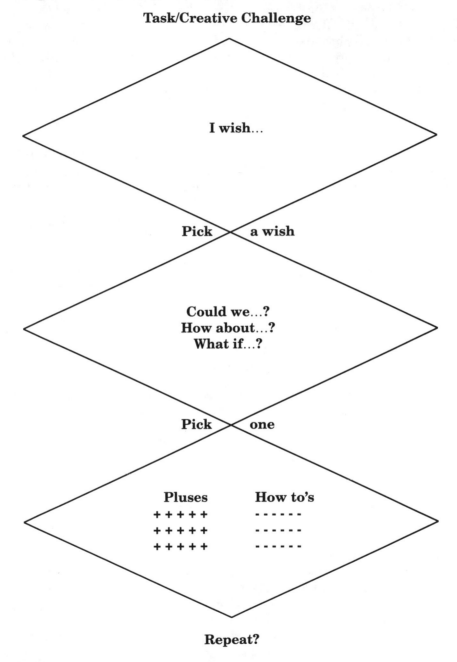

Task/Creative Challenge

I wish…

Pick ✕ **a wish**

Could we…?
How about…?
What if…?

Pick ✕ **one**

Pluses   **How to's**
+ + + +   - - - - - -
+ + + +   - - - - - -
+ + + +   - - - - - -

Repeat?

Next Steps

problem.) If the pluses far outweigh the minuses, you can proceed to an implementation strategy (the final convergence at the bottom of diamond three). If, however, there are two many minuses or challenges to the successful implementation of the idea, you can either go back to the first diamond and start "wishing" new ideas to overcome these minuses or begin the process all over again with a different wish entirely.

Let me give a few quick, real-world examples to demonstrate the power of wishing. Did you know, for instance, that the idea for Disneyland started as a simple wish in Walt Disney's mind that adults could enjoy amusement parks as much as, and right along with, their children. Or that the inspiration for Land's Polaroid camera came from a simple wish/question from his daughter, who wanted to know why she couldn't see the pictures that her father was taking of her right away?

Finally, in a creative session I did for the American Camping Association, I had a particularly difficult camp owner. This fellow had been in the business for more than ten years, and kept saying that he just couldn't imagine creating a camp activity that was new, was affordable, and that the kids would like. So we tried the wish technique. The results were wonderful, as even the skeptical camp owner admitted. One group of wishes that I particularly liked was to have Michael Jordan run a basketball clinic and Madonna give a free concert. Probably not in the camp's budget, right? But as we got to talking about how to approximate these wishes, we discovered a wonderful new camp project: Why not have the kids themselves become their favorite stars? They could make up costumes, give performances, give motivational speeches, or do whatever else they'd imagine their star doing if he or she were to visit the camp. It was a case of "when you wish upon a star, makes no difference who you are, your dreams come true."

■ *Section Five* ■

Applying
Creativity

23

The Great Fish Round-Up: New Product Development Techniques

One of the nice things about new product development work is that unless your parameters are quite narrow, you can generate all kinds of possible solutions. Think about trying to invent a new cereal, or new uses for Velcro, or a new toy or game. You can invent literally anything. Facilitating or participating in these sessions can be wide open—and a lot of fun.

Having worked in new product development for more than fifteen years, and brainstormed new products in everything from hair spray to snack foods, timeless teller machines to children's furniture, frozen desserts to cheeses, children's fruit juices to cold remedies, amusement park rides to financial services, I'd like to share with you several of the most useful and powerful new product development techniques I know.

Setting the Mood: Props, Props, Props

Science fiction writer Ray Bradbury wrote in a room filled with everything from toy dinosaurs to a globe, a bag of marbles to a model of the space shuttle. He used these props to help him get ideas for stories and to trigger creative connections among story elements that he otherwise might not have made. Why not do the same for your creative session?

If you are trying to invent an environmentally safe new form of packaging, why not fill the brainstorming room with exotic plants and play new age background music? If you're looking for futuristic banking concepts, why not put up a picture of the Starship Enterprise?

Do these kinds of props really help the creative process? They certainly do. When Westport, Connecticut, new-product consultant Steve Kaye was asked to help executives of the Life Savers Company invent new flavors, he filled the room with hundreds of flavor ideas, from a list of more than 75+ Baskin-Robbins flavors, to actual samples of exotic fruits (kiwis, kumquats, etc.), to a wide variety of perfume fragrances and scents. Life Savers' highly successful Fruit Juicers line came out of that session.

When Doug Hall, former developer of innovative marketing programs for Procter & Gamble, was trying to invent a new line of cake products for P&G's Duncan Hines division, he filled the room with everything he could imagine to make the session more stimulating and fun. Among his props were greeting cards, which ultimately triggered the idea for Duncan Hines's line of Pantastic® party cakes. Among the party cake themes, complete with specially molded pans and cardboard decorations, are Garfield, Kermit, and Miss Piggy cakes.

You Are the Product

"You are the product" is the role-playing exercise that is especially useful for new product development assignments. Essentially, participants pretend that they are a product, and talk about how being that product makes them feel, act, or perceive the world.

Jim Ferry, a Boston-based innovation consultant, has used "you are the product" to arrive at insights and ideas that, as he says, "you'd be hard-pressed to arrive at through any other method." In one session, for instance, he and his team had executives at Pitney Bowes invent new product ideas for a postage meter by forming a human postage meter, with each executive playing a different part of the machine. As one "part" of the machine put it, "I'm just glad I wasn't the envelope sealer."

In another assignment for the Rich Products Company, the goal was to name a new healthy dessert topping that would be sold to restaurant owners. The team had one person play the dessert, one play the topping, and another play the dessert eater. The dessert said that he "didn't want something too heavy to lift." The topping said that he wanted to be a friend of the dessert, "to get along with him well." And the dessert eater said that he didn't want anything too messy. The name Top Life, to imply a dessert topping for a healthy lifestyle, was the chosen winner.

For the Polymer Technologies Division of Bausch & Lomb, Ferry had executives pair off in teams, with one playing the eyeball and the other playing Bausch & Lomb's rigid gas-permeable contact lens. The eyeball kept asking for a pillow to cushion the hard and "insensitive" contact lens. The result was a new research effort by Polymer to bond a special space-age cushioning material directly onto the contact lens.

Nature's Analogies

When geodesic dome inventor Buckminster Fuller was growing up in Maine, he became frustrated that he could not see where he was going when rowing his boat. One day, he noticed a jellyfish in the water, and it occurred to him that the jellyfish *could* see where it was going. It got him to thinking. Could he invent a similar kind of propulsion system? It wasn't long before he had created a kind of propulsion stick with a collapsible opening and closing umbrella head. When he thrust the head out in the water, the head opened up, pushed water back, and propelled the boat forward. When he pulled the stick back, the head collapsed (creating less drag in the water), and he was ready to start his next round of pushing. So, much like a jellyfish propelling itself through water, or a gondolier pushing his boat through the canals of Venice, he could now see where he was going. A simple, yet effective imitation of nature's genius for invention and design.

Nature can provide a wealth of design ideas, concepts, and inventive approaches to the human side of new product development. I remember, for instance, in one new product session I ran for a manufacturer of steel wool pads, I led the group through a discussion of the benefits and drawbacks of hair to people and animals, and why nature chose to design hair the way it did. Because hair and steel wool have a similar structure and shape (a similarity not lost on the original namer of steel *wool*), I knew that this analogy would give us an entirely different way of thinking about potential uses and markets for a new steel wool product. The result was a new line of *radically* different steel wool cleansing products now under development by the client.

Other examples of nature's influence on product design and invention abound. Probably the best known is that the inspiration for Velcro came from thistle blossoms (burrs) sticking to the pant leg of Swiss inventor Georges de Mestral one day in 1948. Let's look at two lesser-known, but nevertheless intriguing examples from William J. J. Gordon's work with RCA and the West German government.

RCA/Whirlpool came to Gordon in the early 1970s with the assignment of finding a new way to handle home trash. Gordon looked to the animal kingdom for a suitable analogy.

The question he asked himself: How do animals handle their own trash, or, put another way, waste? Who in the animal kingdom handles their waste most efficiently, who less so? Gordon and his co-workers decided that a cow handled waste (at least from the point of view of humans who have to walk through cow pastures) somewhat inefficiently. Goats, on the other hand, are much more efficient. Their waste comes out in a dry, well-contained solid form, much like an encapsulated pellet.

The breakthrough idea: Why not use this idea of encapsulating waste to handle home trash as well? The product that was ultimately marketed was the Trash Masher, the first in a line of appliances we know today as trash compactors.

When another client, the West German government, was looking for a better, more efficient, and more productive way of commercial fishing, they came to Gordon. The conventional solution of simply making larger, stronger, and longer nets had reached an upper limit of sorts. Gordon again looked to nature for an analogy for "netting."

How are animals driven to a specific place for capture? he wondered. How about cattle herding? Or a cattle stampede? What starts a stampede, anyway? Generally a loud noise, like thunder or a gunshot. Is there a way to "stampede" fish to a specific place for an easy "round-up"? Gordon's solution: Use underwater microphones to broadcast threatening noises that act metaphorically as nets to drive the fish to the boats for easy capture. Thus was born the "underwater round-up" solution.

Questioning Assumptions

A useful technique for any kind of problem solving, but particularly useful in a new product development session where you seem to be getting "all the same ideas," is to spend some time questioning your assumptions.

If you were asked to design a new car, for instance, what would some of your most basic assumptions be? That it have four wheels? Or that it have wheels at all? That it be made of metal? That it use gasoline? That you'd need a key to start it? That you'd sit in it (as opposed to, say, lying down in it)? As basic as all these assumptions may seem, every single one of them is now being questioned by the designers of the cars of the future.

In an assignment I worked on to develop a new cereal, some of the assumptions we were making were these:

- Cereal had to be mixed with milk for breakfast.
- Cereal had to be sold in a box.
- Cereal had to be made of some kind of grain.
- Cereal is eaten for breakfast (as opposed to some other time of the day).
- Cereal has to be eaten in a bowl.

As you begin to consider the ramifications of each of these assumptions, new product ideas quickly emerge, don't they? For instance, if cereal doesn't have to come in a box, how else might it be packaged? In a bag, like coffee? Maybe then you could create your own unique brand of cereal (much as people now do at home when they make granola) by combining varying amounts of rice, corn, wheat, oats, raisins, nuts, etc., that are available from large, air-tight bins at the supermarket. Much like fruit, cereal could then be sold by weight. And if you had reusable bags, you'd eliminate the packaging expense (and pollution) altogether, so the cost of your morning bowl of cereal would go down!

The tricky thing about using the questioning assumptions technique is that our assumptions may be so ingrained that even when we consciously try to question them, we can't always see them. In creative terms, familiarity often breeds invisibility. One simple way to get around this is to break this exercise down into two distinct steps.

- List all the facts, elements, attributes, and/or features of the product under consideration.
- Negate, eliminate, or think of the opposite of each of these facts, elements, attributes, and features, and see what you get.

You'll then be in a position to identify even more assumptions you probably didn't even know you were making.

Say, for instance, you make chairs. What are some of the attributes or features of chairs? Arm rests. A seat cushion. Four legs. A back support. A few feet high. Made of wood, plastic, or metal. Try eliminating, negating, or thinking of the opposite of each. Let's examine two of the above features/attributes.

■ ■ ■

1. A chair without armrests? How about a chair without anything, except possibly air, to rest your body on?

Idea A: An antigravity, amusement park "chair" that uses streams of air shot up in specific patterns to create a viable seat.

Idea B (possibly a bit more realistic): An air massage chair that directs streams of hot air through holes in the chair's cushions to whatever part of your tired body needs massaging.

2. A chair is a few feet high. What if a chair were flat?

Idea A: This "chair" is simply a piece of thick padding material that you lay over something else to make it a chair—like a large rock? Why not an all-natural "rock chair"? By the way, did you assume that a chair had to be comfortable?

Idea B: What if the chair were very high—so high, in fact, that you had to stand to use it. Did you assume that chairs were for sitting in? Why not a standing chair?

■ ■ ■

Starting with several features of a chair and negating each one led us to new ways of thinking about the concept of a chair. This, in turn, led us to discover other, even more basic assumptions we might have been making about a chair (a chair should be comfortable, and a chair is for sitting).

One final word of advice: When using this technique, it's very important not to short-circuit seemingly absurd ideas. It's these ideas (e.g., a chair made not for sitting but for standing) that often have the greatest potential. These are the ideas that are least likely to have been considered by your competitors, and that therefore have the potential to lead to a truly original, breakthrough new product concept.

Idea Naming

Have you ever played Hungry, Hungry Hippos®? How about Ants in the Pants®? Or Barrel of Monkeys®? Can you imagine how to play these new action toys simply by hearing their names?

How might you play:

- Winding Blinding Bats!
- Worms that Squirm!
- Shake, Mr. Rattlesnake!
- Hang the Kang-aroo!

Here's how we imagined playing each of these four games:

- *Winding Blinding Bats.* Players try to maneuver wind-up flying bats, suspended from strings tied to poles, into a narrow belfry without breaking off the bat's wings.

- *Worms That Squirm.* Players try to make different-colored earthworms (with magnets in their bellies) squirm their way through an underground passage (also filled with magnets to make the worms "squirm") and reach the "light at the end of the tunnel."

- *Shake, Mr. Rattlesnake.* Parts of several snake's bodies (with one part missing from all but one of the snakes) are put in a special rattle, shaken, and then thrown onto the table. The first team to make a full snake is the winner.

- *Hang the Kang-aroo.* A game from down under! Players try to make their kangaroos "jump up" (by hitting the kangaroo's curved tail, much as you'd hit the prongs of a fork to make it fly off the table) and catch their necks in a noose! (Sick, yes, but kids like sick, right?)

Of course, these are not "real" inventions. But they could have been. How did we create them? Just like you, we started first with the names (which we created, incidentally, by combining an animal in some way with a rhyming verb), then tried to imagine what the game could be based on that name.

As you can see, sometimes just having a name for something can give you an idea. Why not use this as a creative technique to help you invent new products, or even create new marketing or promotion ideas? How?

- Generate two lists of words related to your problem area. List A should be an object or feature, list B an associated action or verb.
- Arbitrarily combine words from list A with words from list B to create two-word names.
- Use the names to prompt ideas.

For example, suppose, your company markets office supplies, and you'd like to generate several new product ideas.
List A could include:

- Scissors
- Rubber band
- Post-it notes
- Memo pad
- White-out

List B could include such office tasks as:

- Filing
- Typing
- Faxing
- Training
- Thinking

Randomly combining lists A and B might suggest such "new products" as:

- *The training pad.* Companywide memo/training/suggestion pads for educating new employees about their company's unique approach to business; they could include the corporate mission statement, quotes from the chairman, goals for the year, customer service tips, etc.

- *Typing scissors.* A bit of a "stretch" here, but how about scissors especially designed (with a special paper-penetrating point) to cut out words (or pictures) from the center of the paper (without having to start cutting from the edge of the paper)?
- *Faxing white-out.* Specially formulated Liquid Paper® white-out that allows you to make changes on documents to be faxed without worrying that it will gum up the works of the fax machine.
- *Post-it™ filers.* Specially formatted Post-it™ notes that allow you to change the name of a file simply by unsticking an old Post-it™ note from the file and sticking on a new one.
- *Rubber band thinking.* A novelty premium called "Mind Stretchers," a box of rubber bands printed with short descriptors of some of history's great ideas.

What's in a name? Sometimes an invention (or two).

━ *24* ━━━━━━━━━━━━━━━

$50 Million and Counting: How to Brainstorm Cost-Cutting Ideas

It was New Years Eve, 1991. Instead of the traditional New Year's Eve party, I thought, wouldn't it be fun to have a New Year's Eve *Resolution* Party? I'd invite our best friends, and we'd all share our goals for the New Year.

It worked out great! We all laughed. We all got to know one another a little better. And we committed publicly to achieving our resolutions—which somehow made them seem more real and important.

One of my goals was to facilitate more different kinds of brainstorming sessions, in part because I knew I'd be writing this book and wanted some unique case histories, and in part to keep my own creative juices flowing.

Imagine my surprise, then, when I got a call—on January 2, no less—asking me to help design and facilitate a series of twenty-five all-day cost-cutting sessions for 300 people (approximately twelve per day) at a billion-dollar personal products company!

The call came from Gerald Haman, president of the Chicago-based firm Creative Learning International, inventor of a unique creativity tool, the Pocket Persuader, and former Procter & Gamble marketing star. Gerald had a client who was looking for ways to uncover—or create—new cost-saving ideas. Since the client had been actively pursuing cost-cutting ideas for the last five years and, as they put it, had already "picked all the low-hanging fruit," it was up to us to design and facilitate a program that would uncover new and innovative ways of cutting costs.

When I began thinking about how to design the session pilot, I knew one thing for sure: Cost-cutting brainstorming sessions would have to be very different from conventional brainstorming sessions. Anyone familiar with brainstorming technique knows that one of the commandments of running a new idea session is to encourage the group to suspend judgment, to try not to be negative about anything. All ideas, no matter how seemingly far out, are good and to be encouraged because often a far-out idea will have a better chance of leading to a truly breakthrough idea than a close-in or sensible idea. Any judgment of ideas is usually postponed to the end of the session, when the group comes to closure and picks the ideas that they feel should be considered for further development.

So why should a cost-cutting idea session be any different? There are several reasons. For one thing, the negatives of a cost-cutting idea need to be considered every step of the way. Otherwise, you have no way of knowing if the idea is any good or not. It's not like a new product or sales situation, where you can get your ideas, develop them, and then go ask the customers what they think. In the case of cost cutting, the employees of the company are the "consumers," and if you don't ask them when you have them there why a cost-cutting idea will or won't fly, you've lost a valuable opportunity to take advantage of their unique expertise, perspective, and experience.

Cost Cutting in the Corporate Culture

The key thing about a cost-cutting idea is that it needs to make sense as an implementable idea within a company's unique corporate culture. A multimillion-dollar cost-reduction idea that could make good sense for one company could be disastrous for another for any number of reasons: corporate politics, effect on company morale, unique marketing environment, competitive factors, etc. The only way to really know if a potential cost-reduction idea is any good or not is to explore the ramifications of actually implementing that idea within the specific company. And that means getting the session participants to tell you the truth—to tell you what they really think (Is it doable or not doable? A good idea or a bad idea? Why or why not?). Then, if they do think it's potentially a good idea, continue brainstorming to overcome any unforeseen obstacles.

Creative cost-cutting sessions also differ from new product development sessions in the number of ideas generated. Some time ago, for instance, I ran a new product development session for a manufacturer of urethane foam in which, in a single day, a group of twelve generated more than 350 new product ideas. In a cost-cutting session, if a group is able to create a half-dozen well- developed and thought-out, implementable ideas, it has done a good day's work.

Also critical to the creative cost-cutting process is assigning dollar values to ideas. This is important for at least three reasons: (1) to help determine if the idea is indeed viable, (2) to help in the ultimate ranking of ideas, and (3) to inspire the group. Without going through a "quick and dirty" cost analysis comparing the idea's potential savings with the expense of actually implementing it, you have no real way of knowing if the idea is any good or not.

By assigning dollar values to ideas, no matter how much of a guesstimate these brainstorming-session dollar values might be, you can also quickly determine an idea's value relative to other cost-saving ideas.

Assigning dollar values also helps the group build a strong sense of achievement and purpose throughout the day. The momentum builds as the group generates ideas worth hundreds of thousands of dollars from a single day of brainstorming. There is a real sense of contribution to the company's financial well-being. Interestingly, we also found a healthy competition developing among groups and departments as word got out about "million-dollar-plus" days of cost-saving ideas. It's one thing to suggest a new idea. It's quite another thing to suggest the same idea, but include the statement, "We estimate this will save the company in excess of $150,000 per year."

So, how did we design the session to uncover or create cost-saving ideas the company had missed? There is a psychological counseling principle that I've never forgotten from my psych major days in college: "You can never fail, when you get to the detail." This simply means that if you can get your patient (or client, as they're now called) to relive past experiences, especially psychologically traumatic experiences, in great detail, much of the repressed pain that accompanied the experience will automatically be triggered and brought back to the surface.

I took a similar tack in structuring the cost-saving session—very much a specific, detailed-oriented, "bottom-up" approach to generating ideas. Start with the mundane details of an employee's everyday job, and see if contained within these everyday work experiences was a specific situation, procedure, or operation that could be generalized into a departmentwide or even companywide cost-saving idea or more efficient way of doing business.

Cutting Costs Through Mind-Mapping

The question was, in a brainstorming session with twelve or so people, what was the easiest and most time-efficient way for each employee to generate the specific details of his or her working day? The best creative technique I know of for this purpose is mind mapping. Mindmapping was invented by Tony Buzan in the mid-1960s. Through a kind of pictorial free association using key words, diagraming-type connectors (remember diagraming in junior high school English?), and symbols, one can quickly do a visual diagram, or map, of virtually any subject you like.

Because of the basic structure of the mind-mapping technique—using free association and symbols—the technique is "right-brain-friendly" and very useful for doing a "brain dump." It's a wonderful way to get literally everything you know about a subject out as quickly as you can, without having to worry about what form the information is taking as it comes out.

So in all our cost-cutting sessions, the first thing I had the members of the group do (after the introductions and warm-up exercises) was mind maps of their jobs—"job maps," if you will. As prompts, I asked them to include on their maps such things as their day-to-day responsibilities, who they reported to, what they did and didn't like about the job, what other departments they worked with—everything.

It was only after everyone completed his or her job map that we went to work finding and developing cost-cutting ideas. With the details of their jobs fresh in their minds, and now on paper in front of them, it was a relatively simple next step to start generalizing from specific problems and inefficiencies into potentially larger, more widely applicable cost-saving ideas.

From the Specific to the General

A good example of this specifics-to-general approach was an idea that came from the job map of an employee in the Hispanic marketing department. One of her responsibilities was to help create displays, header cards, shelf talkers, and other point-of-purchase materials for the Hispanic market. Her job map revealed that she felt she was spending an inordinate amount of time, and therefore possibly wasting money, customizing each P.O.P. piece. In essence, she was having to reinvent the wheel each time a new promotion came along. It was assumed, though, that because the Hispanic market was a specialized market, reinventing the wheel was just one of the costs of doing business in it. As we began to question this assumption, however, she realized that her department could create a series of P.O.P. templates that require only printing changes from one promotion to the next—a low-cost alternative to designing each new P.O.P. piece from scratch. What I found most interesting about this idea, however, was not simply that it was a good idea for her department. As it turned out, *all* the marketing departments were doing exactly the same thing. By adopting her template idea, the company expects to save more than $200,000 per year.

Another intriguing advantage of using the job map technique is that because you literally have a map of the different facets of your job, you can often see relationships between seemingly unrelated problems, costs, and/or opportunities. My favorite surprising relationship story came out of the job maps of a customer service representative and a research executive.

■ ■ ■

The customer service representative was in charge of handling all written customer complaints. As in all companies, a certain very low percentage of defective products makes it through to a consumer. Most customers don't take the time or effort to let the company know about the defect. But a few do. They write to register their dissatisfaction, and ask for a refund. The company gives a full refund, but as the customer service representative's job map revealed, she wanted to do something more. She wanted to figure out a way to turn these dissatisfied customers into loyal users.

The research executive's job map revealed that she was feeling frustrated by the time and cost of finding the right people for the company's consumer research panels.

These two problems were eventually addressed by the same cost-efficient solution: Offer the dissatisfied customers membership in a special "panel of consumer experts" that would provide the company with consumer reactions to ideas for new products and improvements on existing products. In return for their membership, customers would receive free samples, cents-off coupons, inexpensive gifts, and letters of appreciation for taking the time to "be a concerned consumer." The advantage for the research department was that it now had a group of committed, articulate, and often quite well educated customers as part of its market research panels, at a fraction of the normal recruiting cost. The company estimated the idea would save more than $100,000 per year, not to mention the goodwill engendered by turning many of the dissatisfied customers into loyal users. A textbook "win-win" idea.

By the way, in our twenty-five all-day sessions, we generated more than $50 million worth of real-world, start-implementing-them-today cost-saving and quality-improvement ideas.

■ 25

Word Picturing and Associations: How to Be a More Creative Business Presenter, Speaker, and Writer

More than ten years ago, a reporter asked Dick Munro, the then newly appointed president of Time, Inc., about the plans he had for his company. Munro's response, quoted in *The New York Times*, has stayed with me all these years. I'm paraphrasing, but it went something like, "We're not going to rebuild the engine, we're just going to play with the carburetor a little bit."

Instead of using a tired business cliche like "maximize efficiencies," Munro used words that people could relate to—and visualize. He communicated a piece of abstract information—the fact that the company was planning to make only minor changes—in a powerful way with what I call "word pictures."

Using word pictures (technically known as figurative language) to enhance the impact of abstract information is hardly a new idea. Shakespeare called the world "a stage," and Juliet (at least through Romeo's eyes) was the sun. Novelists and journalists have long relied on analogies to give their writing an added measure of color and texture. For example, instead of using the words "rich and dishonest-looking," John McPhee once described a fellow writer as "the kind of man who looks as if he would cheat at polo." Politicians (and their speechwriters) also have recognized the power of a word picture. Think of such memorable phrases as Churchill's "iron curtain" or Bush's "thousand points of light."

As prevalent as they are in literature, journalism, and politics, however, figurative devices are rarely used effectively in business (except, of course, in advertising). And the main reason is, I think, that it takes courage, self-confidence, and creativity to generate powerful word pictures. It's much easier to use the tired, trite, and hackneyed than to create the fresh, compelling, and new.

How can you develop the ability to create your own unique, word pictures? The two best techniques I know of are the magazine cut-and-paste exercise and image streaming (see Chapter 18). Both will help you become more adept at generating and using word pictures. They will stimulate your ability to think visually when you are presenting ideas. They can be especially useful in creating unique and memorable sales presentations, particularly when you need to communicate technical information to a nontechnical audience.

They are useful when you need to write a particularly creative, memorable, or intriguing memo, press release, or even annual report. Banc One Corporation is a good case in point. On the cover of its annual report were beautifully photographed nuts and bolts, with a corresponding "nuts and bolts" tag line. The message was clear: Banc One's phenomenal success is directly related to its knowing and faithfully adhering to the nuts and bolts of the banking business: No glamour—just results.

Robert Frost once said, "an idea is a feat of association." The same could be said of effective word picturing. If you can find a way to link two ostensibly separate worlds and make valid associations between the two, you will be well on your way to writing a piece with impact and memorability.

In the spirit of association, then, look at these excerpts from two trade articles I wrote a few years back, one for an advertising newsletter, the other for a commercial real estate firm.

Advertising Your Genius[1]
Three Rules of Writing Great Ads for Creative Businesses
What Would da Vinci Say?

The year: 1492. And Leonardo da Vinci was in a fix. Times were tough at court and he needed to drum up additional "business" (patrons). But how? It's not easy telling the world you're talented—much less a genius.

Da Vinci decided to write to His Excellency Ludovic Sforza to promote his considerable talents. Interestingly, the style and substance of his letter exemplified three important and timeless rules of advertising creative services.

Rule #1: Present your talents in light of a current market need. Did da Vinci say that he was a great artist? Or that he was the best "mirror writer" in all of Italy? No, he identified a pressing need, and offered to fill it: namely to design and build "instruments of war" for His Excellency.

Rule #2: Be specific about your creative point of difference. Da Vinci's letter noted that he had studied the work of other "masters and inventors of instruments of war"—and found that their work did not "differ in any respect from those in common practice." He went on to outline how his unique, easy-to-transport "unassailable armored cars and catapults of wonderful efficacy"[2] were superior to anything yet invented.

Rule #3: Use more "you's" than "I, me, my or we's" in your headline. This is the acid test for Rule #1: Make sure you're focusing not on yourself—but on the needs of your potential client(s). Da Vinci's opening paragraph, for instance, had four "you and Your Excellency's" and only three "I, me, my or we's."

Not bad, right? But can you also generate compelling word pictures and associations if you have to write, say, a highly technical or industry-specific piece on labor negotiations, or TQM, or high-tech manufacturing? Yes. You just may have to work a little harder at finding appropriately compelling images to make your points. I guarantee you, though, that it'll be worth the effort, not only for your reader, but for you as well.

Let's look at a fairly technical (and, in my opinion, potentially deadly dull) subject: loss factors in office buildings. See if this word-picture/association treatment I did of the topic for a real estate trade magazine doesn't at least pique your interest.

The Case of the 13-Inch Ruler[3]

Detective Sam Space needed a place to hang his hat (and locate his business), but it was becoming a tough case to crack.

It wasn't that there weren't enough office buildings to choose from. Just the opposite. It was a big town. The kind of town that could swallow you up and spit you out. There were too many buildings; 50 in all. How to choose the right one? That was the question.

Like any good detective, Sam began with the facts. Was the parking adequate? The views? The elevators? Would the air conditioning keep Sam cool during those sultry summer nights he'd have to work late? How about the hallways? Would his clients think his office was classy enough?

The list of possible spaces dwindled. Finally, only five cut the mustard. But that's when it got tough. Really tough. How to choose the right one? The wrong choice could be, well, deadly.

Like a bad hangover, it came to him. The ransom, that's how he'd decide. Whichever landlord wanted the least amount of rent money, see, that's the one he'd go with; all other things being equal, why not?

The bids came in: $18 per square foot, then $19 and $19

again. Some joker walked in with $20 and another with $21. No contest. Sam'd go with the $18 space. Case closed.

Or was it? Had Sam made a fatal mistake?

Could it be that the $21 per square foot property was actually a better deal than the one priced at $18 per square foot? In fact, it was! Sam hadn't stopped to consider the *thirteen-inch ruler!*

What is a thirteen-inch ruler? It's our way of pointing out that all landlords—surprising as it may seem—do not measure their space the same way. A square foot of office space in one building may be more or less than a square foot in another. How? The difference is in usable versus rentable square feet.

Usable square feet, as you might guess, is the amount of space that your company will be occupying; in essence the amount of space that you will actually be able to use. Rentable square feet, on the other hand, is the amount of space your company will *actually be paying rent on*—and this amount of space is always more than the amount of usable square feet.

The reason for this difference is that the square footage of all the common areas within the building—lobbies, elevators, hallways, etc.—is divided up among all the tenants, and paid for by them on a pro-rated basis. In the industry, this is known as the loss factor.

As a rule of thumb, loss factors range from 9 percent to 14 percent in efficient, well-designed office buildings for single-floor tenants.

The article went on to give a detailed description of loss factors, and the client's recommendations for making sure you weren't comparing apples to oranges.

My final bit of advice: The more apples and oranges (word pictures) you can bring into your business presenting, speaking, and writing, the better off you and your audience will be!

Notes

1. Bryan Mattimore, "Advertising Your Genius," *The Innovator,* Vol. 3, No. 1, 1992, p. 3.
2. Edward MacCurdy, narr. and trans., *The Notebooks of Leonardo da Vinci* (New York: Reynal & Hitchcock, 1939), pp. 1152–1153.
3. Bryan Mattimore, "The Case of the 13-Inch Ruler," *Intercorp,* Vol. 8, No. 12, 1989, p. 7.

26

Not Giving Up the Ghost: The Art of Naming

A good name should be available, pronounceable, and translatable; have lasting utility; lend itself to graphic representation; communicate a product's unique selling proposition; and capture the essence of why the product is right for a particular segment of the consuming public. Quite a tall order for what often comprises just one or two words, isn't it?

After you've tried "every" conceivable combination from your dictionary, thesaurus, and rhyming dictionary (for the third time), and it begins to look as if that single best name just does not exist, thoughts often turn to finding a compromise solution. The finite nature of words is imposing its limits on the infinity of creative thought. This is the danger point in any naming assignment, and it's the reason for this chapter. For those who don't wish to compromise, what follows is a list of six approaches to creative name generation that you might use to help you break "namer's block." Of the more than 100 new product and company naming assignments on which I have worked, each approach, at one time or another, has helped me break through to a new and innovative naming solution.

Strike the Chord of Familiarity

Given the high cost of establishing a brand name, sometimes a good way to approach a naming assignment—from the standpoints of both creativity and marketing—is to look for a name that already has some kind of built-in recognizability. Generally, consumers are more responsive to a name that has an element of familiarity to it. It's human nature to have

Portions of this chapter originally appeared in Bryan W. Mattimore, *The Art of Naming*, CHEMTECH, Vol. 18, June 1988, pp. 328–330.

a greater level of trust in something you know than in something you don't.

I once adopted this tactic of familiarity to invent and subsequently name a new card game called Ghost, based on the well-known dinner table word game. The Trademark Office granted me a supplemental registered trademark on the Ghost name, and ultimately I was able to license it to Milton Bradley for the board game Ghosts.

A less direct connection, but one that still found its inspiration in the strike-the-chord-of-familiarity principle, was the naming of the most successful new doll of the 1980s. Whether American consumers were aware of it or not, the genesis, in part, of the Cabbage Patch concept was an ancient European superstition that girls were born inside pink roses, and boys were found under (of all things) cabbages.

Of course, striking the chord of familiarity is not limited to the naming of dolls or games, or even movie sequel titles, for that matter. In an assignment for a national bakery company, I was asked to name a new, healthier triangle-shaped cracker. The client wanted two kinds of names to test: one that said "upscale"/more expensive, and another that said lower cost/more mainstream. In both the names I proposed, I tried to strike the chord of familiarity by associating the cracker's unique shape with a known entity. For the upscale positioning, the cracker reminded me of a sail, and so we called it Spinnakers. For the mainstream positioning, I had been thinking about the success of Pepperidge Farm's Goldfish crackers, and I suddenly realized that this cracker looked like an Angelfish!

So which name did the client choose? Neither, unfortunately. Before we got to test the names, consumer research revealed that our healthy cracker had a problem with its shape. Consumers were worried that they might choke on the points of the triangles. The project quickly lost the wind from its sails.

Finally, striking the chord of familiarity may be as subtle as using a few of the same letters and adapting a graphic "look" or design from something else. Consider the story behind one of the most expensive name changes ever undertaken: the switch in the early 1970s from Esso to Exxon.

■ ■ ■

Like many naming assignments these days, this one began with a computer search. Hundreds of names were generated, many beginning with *E* to maintain some identification with the "old" Esso name. Unfortunately, none of the computer's creations tested well. After months of unsuccessful testing, the problem was, in part, solved—not by a computer but by a secretary who found a way to strike the chord of familiarity.

"What" she asked, "is the most commonly seen sign in America?"

"FREE?" "MEN'S ROOM?" "NEW?" After some hemming and hawing, one of the executives present looked down the hall to his office, and said finally, EXIT.

"Why not use part of the word EXIT in your name?" said the secretary. "Maybe, say, the word EXON?"

Shortly thereafter, with the addition of a graphically compelling *X*, the name Exxon was born.

Does this story sound apocryphal? I have it on good authority that it's not. But if you have any doubt, don't take my word for it. Next time you go by your local Exxon station, just notice the EXXON letters. Blocked and red as they are, they look suspiciously like (you guessed it) an EXIT sign.

Find the Essence

Lost as we get in the world of words, we often lose sight of exactly what we want our name to communicate. Sometimes it's useful to step back and ask yourself two of marketing's most basic questions: What makes your product or service unique, and who is your market? If you're not absolutely clear on how to answer these questions, often you'll find yourself creating names that "just don't feel right" because intuitively you know that they're communicating the wrong message and/or positioning. Conversely, when you very clearly know your market and what makes your product or service unique, that focus, like a well-aimed arrow, can lead you to a naming bull's-eye rather quickly.

Think about Nabisco's vanilla sandwich cookie Giggles. What do you remember as the essence of your lunchroom eating experience in elementary school? I can't help but see my silly, goofy, laughing, giggly classmates shooting spitballs, throwing cold mashed potatoes across the room, and spitting out warm milk into their jello. When I remember how lunchtimes were, calling a cookie Giggles, and even adding a baked-in smile to the "face" of the cookie, seems to me the essence of great naming.

Another good example of "essence naming" is the highly successful product Success Rice. When Robert Homan's New York–based New Products Resources did research on boxed rice, they discovered that consumers wanted a quick, foolproof way to make delicious rice. With the then-new boil-in-the-bag technology, this had become possible. Unconventional as it was, they gave the product a name that captured the essence of what consumers were saying they wanted when preparing their rice: success.

Of course, finding the essence of your naming assignment is not always easy. As with many creative ideas, the answer may seem obvious in retrospect. But this doesn't make discovering it any easier. On an assignment to name an environmental book club for a well-known publishing house, for instance, I struggled for weeks trying to find the essence of what I wanted the name to convey. But it wasn't until I saw a road sign that said ELM STREET that I suddenly realized what the naming assignment was all about. The name of the book club should communicate a sense of nature (elm) in balance with civilization (street). Once I had made this positioning discovery, it was relatively easy to generate a half-dozen on-target, winning names.

I guess in this case finding the essence was a combination of dogged determination and keeping the problem top of mind until somewhere, somehow, something triggered the answer.

Find the Visual

As right-brained art directors know, many creative marketing problems are solved by finding the appropriate visual. The same visual approach to problem solving can be applied to the decidedly left-brain, language oriented goal of finding a new product name. If you can find the appropriate picture, the single best name may quickly follow.

I once worked on the naming of a new sore throat sprayer. This carry-anywhere, use-anytime sore throat medication was packaged in an innovative spray bottle that let you spray medication directly to the sore spot in your throat. For the spray to hit its target, the user's mouth had to be opened fairly wide. In a moment of reverie, thinking of the opened mouth somehow elicited an image of a lion tamer sticking his head inside the wide-open mouth of a lion. The name "Throat Tamer: to soothe the 'roar' of sore throat pain" was not far behind.

A copywriter friend of mine had a similar visual naming experience. He was asked to name a new candy bar that was unique because of its white chocolate covering and red stripes. The look of the bar brought to his mind a picture of an animal with stripes, and eventually he named it White Tiger.

How can you find the appropriate visual? Visuals, in and of themselves, obviously are everywhere. On TV, in magazines, in books. Everything we see in the outside world. Everything we can imagine (or remember) in our inside world. Visuals indeed are everywhere. So, much like the process of essence finding, discovering the right visual can be a rather random, hit-or-miss process. Ultimately, success comes from a combination of the namer's motivation and determination, attention, synchronicity, and/or luck. The key, though, is to be ready when the visual appears.

It's a mysterious process. And, frankly, the only advice I can give for working within the confines of the mystery is in the form of a metaphor. Try to make sure that the receiving station of your mind is constantly "on-line," ready to accept the visual transmissions that the world is sending you. Sooner or later, locked within one of those transmissions will be the solution to your naming assignment. And when that happens, suddenly you will indeed see that a picture has been worth a thousand words!

Watch, Read, and Listen

An allied approach to finding the visual is what I call the watch, read, and listen approach. Essentially, this strategy is to words what the find the visual strategy is to pictures. Again you need to be paying attention to the outside world. (Sometimes the creative person, trying as he or she is to pull the solution from within, may miss those external stimuli that in some mysterious way can supply a creative solution.) Television, the newspapers, a word spoken in conversation are all sources of inspiration.

A wonderful naming story is told by Al Coleman, an advertising man assigned the task of naming a new cooking pot from Rival Manufacturing Co. While watching TV one night, he heard a news commentator use the term "crackpot." That night, at 1:30 A.M., while he was sleeping, the idea hit him. Why not name this new product, which actually was made of crockery and shaped like a pot, the Crock Pot?

And speaking of sleeping, one of America's best-known sleep aids was named by a fellow listening to his "outside" world. While walking home from the office late one night, this fellow, stumped for a name, noticed a group of women leaving the theater. They bid adieu to one another by saying, " 'Night, all; 'night, all." This alert idea man had his name: Nytol.

Next time you're stuck for a name and feel locked into a particular way of thinking, listen to the radio, read a good book, or try writing down interesting words you see used in *The New York Times*. I promise you, at the very least, a mind-opening experience.

Adapt a Principle

Lean Cuisine, Dry Idea, Slimfast, Sunkist, Cool Whip, Hamburger Helper, Taster's Choice, Lexus—great names all. But why? What makes them great?

Most creative people, whether they know it consciously or not, have a wonderful hobby: They collect principles. What was it about that movie that made it so enjoyable? What makes one product's positioning so much better than another's? Why is a particular novel such a good read? For those who collect principles, creative problem solving can become an enormously fun game of adapting a principle to fit an entirely different set of creative problems. Naming is no exception. When you analyze what makes a great name great, you can't help but discover naming principles that might help you solve your particular naming assignment.

What makes L'Eggs such a wonderful name for pantyhose? Beyond, of course, telling you what the product is for, it uses the provocative naming strategy of linking the name directly with the product package, an egg-shaped plastic container. So, how might you use this same strategy to name a new self-heating sink powder that "blasts away stains and grease"? You might call it Powder Keg, and package it in a keglike container.

What naming principle is inherent in the doggie treat Snausages? It contains an interesting strategy of combination, bringing together the words "snack" and "sausages" in one name. We see a similar strategy of combination being used to name the game Pictionary ("picture dictionary") and Swatch ("Swiss watch").

I was once asked to name a new product reporting service. There have been many such services on the market with rather forgettable names, like *The New Product Newsletter, New Products and Processes,* and *Innovation News.* I wanted my name to "cut through," to be both memorable and innovative. I looked to other successful names for a transferable principle. The information search company FIND/SVP (SVP stands for *s'il vous plaît*) provided the answer. I applied its acronymic approach to naming and created *The P.O.I.N.T. Report,* which stood for Profit Opportunities in New Technologies.

Looking for the naming principles inherent in other successful names and then applying these principles to your own naming problem is one of the most effective ways I know of to create a great name without a great deal of effort.

What's the Opposite?

Sometimes it makes sense to do exactly the opposite of what everyone else is doing. It's an interesting way to think, often yielding surprisingly effective and memorable naming results. Apple Computer, of course, selected its decidedly friendly name, in contrast to those of the rest of the industry, to imply its ease of use. And who could ever forget the car rental companies that named themselves Rent-A-Wreck and Ugly Duckling?

Reebok is another interesting example of reverse psychology. What a strange-sounding name for a sneaker. On the surface, it seems to make no sense, except for possibly unconsciously communicating the word 're-bound," or possibly "bebop." Surprisingly, it's memorable and powerful, sounding more high tech and more current than, say, Converse or Keds. Where did the name Reebok come from? It's not high tech at all; reebok is the name of a swift, fleet-footed African gazelle.

Where will the elusive new product or new company name come from? There are no easy answers, and it takes persistence to give birth to that truly creative idea. If you're not sure whether you've got the name or not, a rule of thumb is that you don't. Continue searching. When you finally find it, you'll know it. It'll be obvious. You'll wonder why you didn't think if it sooner, and above all, you'll be excited about it. And if you ever find yourself faltering in your search for that perfect name, I hope you'll find inspiration in the stamina of the Greek runner Pheidip-pides, who at the finish of his run from Marathon uttered but one word, the name of the Greek goddess of victory, Nike.

■ 27 ━━━━━━━━━━━━━━━

The Process of Process Reengineering: Designing a Brainstorming Session

"It's a Fortune 500 company. Thirty-five of their top managers will be flying in from around the country for a day and a half process reengineering and quality improvement brainstorming session. Would you like to work with us to design and facilitate the session?" Louise Korver, president of the Greenwich, Connecticut, firm Corporate Learning & Development, wanted to know.

"Yes, I would," I responded.

With companies facing the seemingly impossible task of cutting costs while also improving quality and service, process reengineering has become a critical component of successful business practice in the 1990s. Process reengineering, originally an engineering and manufacturing term for simplifying and improving the efficiency, design, and manufacture of products, has come to include the improvement and redesign of all manner of company management and service practices.

On this particular assignment, we were asked to help reengineer a chemical company's innovative new distribution system. Specifically, this company had pioneered the use of returnable containers for its chemicals, and was looking for ways to improve the distribution, collection, and tracking of these containers. Personnel from every department were assembled to brainstorm how to reengineer the process to make it more efficient, user-friendly, simple, and cost-effective. Without getting into the specific content of the session itself, I thought it might be useful to the reader to see the overall design of a process reengineering brainstorming session as well as to understand the rationale for the specific exercises in that session.

It's important to recognize that literally weeks of planning went into the design of this session. The exercises we ultimately selected (from among the more than two dozen we considered) were included to meet very well-defined and specific business objectives. Among the criteria we used to design and select the included exercises were considerations of group size, participant experience with brainstorming (limited), participant thinking styles (as a whole, quite process-oriented), stated corporate and session objectives, and time of day. We also spent a considerable amount of time deciding in what order, and for what length of time, each exercise should be presented for maximum effect and result. Much as an Olympic gymnast might envision each and every move of a routine before giving the actual performance, we visualized the steps and anticipated results for each and every exercise to make sure that the exercise contributed to the objectives of the overall session. Paradoxically, it's the best-planned sessions that allow the greatest free flow of "unplanned" creative problem-solving ideas to emerge.

Day 1: How Things Are

Day one of the two-day session ran from 12:30 P.M. to 6:30 P.M. Lunch was brought in. The first forty-five minutes of the session included a welcome, expectations and goals, introductions, and several creative warm-up and team-building exercises. At 1:15, we got down to specific reengineering work.

In order to reengineer or improve a process, it's a good idea first to clearly understand that process as it now exists. Exercise one, therefore, was to create a detailed visual representation or "process map" of each step in the process. We did this by simply recording the details of each step on flip chart paper and posting the lists around the room. The order of the steps was determined by the life cycle of the container itself, from initial manufacture to return for recycling. Problems in the process were duly noted, but no effort was made to solve these problems. That would come later. For now, we were simply trying to understand and visualize the overall process. This process mapping exercise took an hour and a half and was followed by a ten-minute break.

At 3:00 P.M. we randomly assigned the participants to three breakout groups for a series of customer role-playing exercises. Since there were primarily three groups of "customers" along the distribution chain, we had each of the three groups pretend that it was one of the customers, essentially acting as a focus group to record its perceptions and give us an objective view—both good and bad—of the returnable container program. We included this exercise to help the participants get "outside themselves" and their specific roles in the process, and begin to empathize with the concerns, needs, and priorities of their *customers*. We hear so much about customer orientation these days. This role-playing exercise was a very effective way to move beyond simply paying lip service to customer concerns and create a true feeling of empathy and identification among the on-line service providers. At 3:45, the three groups re-assembled and reported their findings.

At 4:30 (after a fifteen-minute break), the group was randomly divided into two groups for a competitive teams exercise. Each team was given the specifications for one of two new products ostensibly designed by rival research and development departments within their company. The new products were intended to offer a kind of competitive brand insurance against the likelihood that their currently marketed product (the one group was there to process reengineer) would some day lose market share to an outside competitor.

The wrinkle was that only one of the two proposed new products would be funded by management. Each team was therefore given the assignment of creating a presentation for the company's board of directors that would convince the board to fund its product over the other team's. (Each of the two new products, incidentally, was given an imagined name along with detailed product specifications before being assigned to a team.) We allowed each team an hour and a half to create a presentation. At 6 P.M. sharp, each group took ten minutes to make its presentation to a fictional board of directors (actually three of the company's top marketing people). The winner was to be announced the next morning, with each winning team member receiving "valuable prizes."

This turned out to be a tremendously successful exercise for several reasons:

- It helped management anticipate potential new product introductions from actual competitors.
- It helped each team member understand the strengths and weaknesses of the company's current product's manufacturing and distribution system.
- It suggested ways to strengthen the product's manufacturing and distribution system by considering other product innovations.
- It took advantage of the competitive spirit of the team members and turned what often is a low-energy time (the end of the day) into a high-energy, exciting, and worthwhile exercise for the company and the participants.

Day 2: How Things Could Be

Day two began at 8:00 A.M. with an announcement of the previous night's winners. Both teams, as it turned out, did such an extraordinary job that senior management awarded everyone prizes.

After a creative warm-up exercise and a quick review of the previous day's results, we formally began day two's activities with a problem identification exercise, since a critical first step in creative problem solving is to clearly define what problem it is you're trying to solve. You'd be surprised how often groups, after several hours of brainstorming, discover that they've been trying to solve the wrong problem.

Three teams were randomly formed and given the assignment of identifying which problems they thought were the most critical. Teams were given forty-five minutes to select and rank their choices. The groups were then given another thirty minutes (ten minutes for each group) to report on their decisions. Finally, using a group decision technique called "dot voting," the group as a whole came to a consensus as to which problems to work on. (See page 169.)

With a break, this took us to 10:15 A.M. Now, with the problems clearly identified and ranked in terms of priorities, it was time to begin actual problem solving. I spent the next forty-five minutes training the group in three simple, yet powerful, creative problem-solving techniques: mindstorming, brainwriting, and wishing diamonds. (See page 109.) In each case, I demonstrated how to apply the technique by actually using it to solve one of the identified problems.

Mindstorming and Brainwriting

Mindstorming is an individual creative technique that involves simply writing down a pre-determined number of ideas for solving any given problem. Simple as it sounds, it is a surprisingly effective technique. Typically, when we try to solve a problem, we settle for the first "really good idea" that comes along. Rarely do we try to generate more ideas, especially when the first idea truly does solve the problem. When you have to generate a predetermined number of ideas or solutions, however, you can't stop with the first good idea that comes up. You've got to keep going until you reach your goal (I find ten to be a good idea goal for beginners, twenty for more experienced ideators). The technique forces quality out of quantity. Interestingly, many of the best and most imaginative ideas occur at the end of the exercise, at ideas 8, 9, and 10. Why? I think it's a combination of sometimes getting the old or obvious ideas out first and a tendency for people to allow themselves to entertain farther-out (even sillier) ideas at the end of the exercise as they try to reach their goal.

The second technique, brainwriting, is a great technique when you have a lot of people in a session and would like to generate a ton of ideas very quickly. The way it works: Divide your large group into smaller groups of, say, five people each. Each person then writes down a thought or creative suggestion on a piece of paper. Then each person passes the paper on to the next person, who writes down a follow-up suggestion based on what the first person has said. The papers are passed again and again until everyone has had a chance to write on all the papers and each person has gotten his or her original paper back. It's fast moving, fun, very stimulating—and generates literally hundreds of ideas in a very short time. It also gets everyone involved in a nonthreatening way: It's much easier to write down a "silly" idea than to say it in front of thirty other people. An added plus is that the technique can easily be adapted to a companywide brainstorming session by using networked computers.

Problem solving lasted through lunch until 1:00. At 1:00, we asked each group to prioritize its solutions and prepare to give a verbal report of its ideas to the group as a whole at 1:30. From 1:30 to 2:00, we had reports.

As it turned out, the group generated—as I'd hoped we would— more ideas than we knew what to do with. We spent the rest of the day (from 2:00 to 3:45) grouping the ideas, prioritizing them, and creating action plans for each high-priority idea, including who was responsible for doing what, when, and with what desired outcome.

If you're wondering how we prioritized so many ideas with such a large group, we used a simple four-box grid (see Figure 3). The two main criteria we used to separate and group ideas were (1) easy versus hard to do and (2) high versus low customer visibility. This was a quick and very effective way to bring the group to closure and help company executives decide which ideas were the most important to begin implementing immediately.

Figure 3. A simple four-box grid.

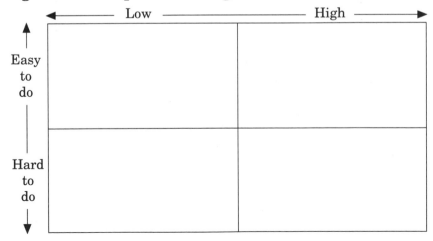

■ 28

Humor Me! The Creation and Uses of Business Humor

Steve Cony used to be vice-president of a major New York bank.

Steve Cony used to be vice-president of a major New York ad agency.

Steve Cony is now a "motivational humorist."

A what? As president of a four-year-old, Croton-on-Hudson, New York, firm Communication Counselors, Steve gives talks and seminars on the strategic uses of humor in business. Let's listen in on one of his talks.

■ ■ ■

You must understand. There is a tremendous difference between comedy and humor. Comedy is about creating jokes, and 90 percent of all jokes are mean-spirited. Humor, on the other hand, uses anecdotes about you and your life, real-life experiences that make you laugh. Not many of us are comedians. But all of us are funny.

Let's look at some of the benefits and uses of humor for the business manager looking to achieve specific business goals. There are at least six. Humor can be used: (1) as a way to "break the ice" in stiff, or uncomfortable business situations, 2) as an effective bonding technique, a wonderful way to build common ground with other employees, (3) as a way to break down resistance to your own point of view, (4) as a much-needed way to improve the content, enjoyment, and ultimately the productivity of meetings, (5) as a way to assign work when people "can't take any more," and (6) as a wonderful way to ease and control tension.

And what about the personal benefits of humor to the business manager? These include: (1) a way to relieve stress, (2) a way to achieve a more positive perspective on a particular assignment or setback, (3) a way to advance your career— people like to work with people they like and can have fun

with, and (4) a way to help you out of tight spots or very negative circumstances.

■ ■ ■

A good example of this last point was a situation that came up with
a traffic manager whom Steve supervised at his ad agency. The traffic
manager, Brian, it seems, had forgotten to mail a critical piece of artwork
that Steve had promised the client "yesterday." Needless to say, Steve was
not happy. Brian's response (delivered with deadpan seriousness): "I have
one foolproof way to remedy this problem. I quit."

"Over the years, Brian must have quit a thousand times," says Steve,
"but each time he quit, I couldn't help but laugh. He helped me see the
absurdity of taking myself too seriously."

Take your job as seriously as you can, but don't take yourself too
seriously—good advice for the business manager in search of a long-lost
sense of humor. Another way to come to one's "senses of humor" is, as
Cony suggests, to build up a "humor folder."

"Since humor is and should be a legitimate and valuable tool in business, doesn't it make sense to spend some time developing and sharpen-
ing this tool? A humor folder will do this."

And what should you put in this folder? "Anything that makes you
laugh," says Cony.

■ ■ ■

When a businessperson hears or thinks of something important, what is the first thing he or she does? Writes it down.
Why should humor be any different? When something funny
happens to you, write it down, just a quick note, even just a
word to remind you of the experience, and then put it in your
humor folder. You never know when you'll be able to use that
anecdote to build a relationship with a co-worker, deflect an
attack from a disgruntled co-worker, or break the ice with a
new business prospect.

We become that which we choose to put our attention on.
To find your humor, start noticing and looking for it. That's the
way to rediscover it inside yourself.

■ ■ ■

Cony also recommends putting cartoons in your humor folder, especially those that might in some way relate to your co-workers, your department, your company, your industry, or business in general. "You
never know when that meeting cartoon from *The New Yorker* might be just
the cartoon you're looking for to set the stage for a particularly important
meeting," says Cony.

And what is the most effective kind of humor? "Self-deprecating humor. People intuitively know that it's a sign of self-confidence when

someone is willing to make light of himself. There is also no faster way of building trust and intimacy with another person than by your willingness to poke a little fun at yourself," says Cony.

Humor in Your Meetings and Brainstorming Sessions

The best meetings and brainstorming sessions are filled with energy and excitement. They are also, at times, playful and fun.

One of the funniest, most exciting, and most playful (and productive) brainstorming sessions I ever attended was with a group of comedy writers at the American Comedy Network. I'd like to tell you about this session because I think it represents an ideal of creative openness and risk taking in meetings and brainstorming sessions to which we all can aspire. (And who knows, maybe you'll even get something you can add to your humor folder.)

The American Comedy Network has its headquarters in Bridgeport, Connecticut. Each week the company writes and produces a thirty-minute comedy package that is syndicated to more than 250 radio stations across the nation. The package includes comedy skits and song parodies on current events, politicians, TV, the movies, etc. Some of the regular characters (in part because the company has actors that do a good job of imitating them) are Barney Fife (of Mayberry RFD); Ralph Kramden of the Honeymooners; Tom BrokeJaw, anchor person; Mr. Ed; and of course, the President of the United States, usually sounding like pretty much of an idiot.

I had been invited to attend the weekly brainstorming session because, well, I asked. I had read about this company in a local newspaper, and I was curious about how a group of people could, week-in, week-out, meet the creative demands of writing and producing a half hour of comedy. I knew that creatively they must have figured out a system, and I was curious about what this system might be. I was also interested in what kinds of people chose to write comedy for a living. Most of all, though, I was interested in how they ran their creative sessions. I felt I might learn something that could help me in my own facilitating work.

And so I drove the half hour from my office to Bridgeport to attend their weekly brainstorming session.

When I arrived at the American Comedy Network's offices, there was no receptionist, so I walked back to where I heard laughter. I peeked into the second door on the right and saw twelve thirty-something gals and guys all dressed in David Letterman creative casual—Reeboks, khakis, jeans, comfortable cotton shirts.

I walked in to the room and waited for someone to ask if they could help me. And you know what? No one did. For at least twenty seconds, I just stood there, and conversations continued as before. I was neither included nor excluded. It just seemed that no one wanted to bother with having to say, May I help you? In a way, I kind of liked it.

Finally I said, "Is Maggie Duggan here?"

Up pops a preoccupied Maggie Duggan, attractive, with short blond hair, very bright, exuding an aura of open confidence and focused, goal-oriented energy, the thirty-year-old president of the American Comedy Network. She greeted me warmly.

The group had a nice feel to it—no egomaniacs, mutual respect; directed and balanced. These people seemed pretty well adjusted. I guess I'd assumed that to be any good, comedy writers (if you believe the Mel Brooks stories) would have to be at least a little weird, if not bouncing off the walls, or somehow cast in the stream of life with not a whole lot of paddles among them. Not so. These were normal, self-actualizing, creative risk takers, seemingly embracing life (or maybe devouring life would be a better way to put it).

"Welcome, Bryan. We're just about to start the brainstorming session. Can I get you coffee or a bagel or something?"

"I'm all set, thanks."

Maggie directed my attention to a handmade poster, taped high up on the office window, with a title that read, "The Rules O' Brainstorming," and six rules below:

- Defer judgment.
- Free-wheel; be outrageous.
- Quantity of ideas more important than quality.
- Combine ideas.
- Write down every idea.
- Every idea/person is valuable.

I gave a knowing nod, and Maggie began the session. She began it the way she begins every session, with a question: "So what's going on in the news?"

It didn't take long before the room was buzzing. "Infomercials are big. Tony Robbins and Fran Tarkenton. The Juiceman. Could we do some kind of infomercial for kids? Maybe sell silly condoms instead of Silly Putty?"

"How about a new channel—the Dysfunctional Channel—you could call in for products only dysfunctional people use."

"Like what, whips and chains?"

"What about the those 900 numbers . . . where you call up sex kittens or . . . or sports guys . . . or psychics?"

"What about a 900 number where you could call to talk to Satan or one of his 'messengers'? Jeffrey Dahmer or maybe Ted Bundy?"

"A 666 number!" Todd Cummings, the head writer, starts imitating Satan in a voice reminiscent of *The Exorcist,* or Darth Vader, or maybe even Bob Guccione. "Hello. Satan speaking; may I help you?"

"What else have we got?"

"Vampires are getting kind of big, aren't they? How about a dyslexic vampire?"

"I want to bluck your sud?" says one of their hottest writers, Nancy Parker, who's also a successful stand-up comic.

"Could we give him a lisp too?" adds another writer.

"Marilyn Monroe is hot too. How about if we had Tom Brokejaw do a Giraldo-opening-Al-Capone's-vault kind of thing? Have Brokejaw do a report from the grave."

"Yea, Brokejaw could 'jump Marilyn's bones.'"

"How about a song parody of Abraham, Martin, and John, only make it Marilyn, Bobby, and John?"

■ ■ ■

And so it went. What I found most amazing about this group was not so much the quality of the ideas (which was obviously very high), but how quickly they popped out. In the best brainstorming sessions, ideas flow fast and furious, and I was certainly used to this rapid pace in new product development and advertising sessions, but in comedy, it was hard to keep up. I wanted to bask in the laughs of each new idea, but before I knew it we were on to the next one. Equally amazing was that often the writers would perform their ideas:

"How about some sexual tension between Wilbur and Mr. Ed?" Then you'd hear the writer do a very passable imitation of Mr. Ed, saying, "Oh Wiiiilllllburrrrr, what are you doing in my stall again?" in his inimitable horse talk—and then, before you knew it we'd be on to the next idea.

In my opinion, the brainstorming sessions I attended at ACN (I went back for another one) were an example of the very best in brainstorming technique, a worthy goal for any business brainstorming facilitator. There were several factors at work here.

For one, you had very strong and self-confident personalities. These people were not afraid to look foolish. After all, most of their ideas *didn't* work. I think it's especially courageous to risk presenting a new idea while doing an impersonation or impression to boot. You can look doubly foolish if the idea's a lousy one.

Equally incredible, I think, was their willingness to risk looking foolish not only with their co-writers, people they knew and presumably were comfortable with, but with an outsider as well. And not just any outsider, but someone who was going to be writing about what they were doing! Again, this takes a tremendous amount of self-confidence.

Facilitator Duggan also kept the session moving. After only an hour and a half, the group had generated close to sixty comedy concepts. Because of the experience and professionalism of the writers, they were willing to go right along with their facilitator and not get bogged down in details. The goal of this meeting was to get as many ideas out as quickly as possible. Everyone knew there'd be time to write the specifics of each skit later. Right now they were looking for the big ideas. How much better would most of our meetings in business be if we focused primarily on the search for big ideas and left the detail work to much smaller teams or groups later?

So what can the business manager in search of better meetings and brainstorming sessions learn from the American Comedy Network? A few suggestions:

- When you've got an important creative assignment, get your very best, most self-confident co-workers to help you. Even one "stick in the mud" can bog your session down.
- Try to involve these self-confident co-workers in an ongoing effort. The more you can work with the same group of people, the more everyone will begin to trust one another and feel confident about taking creative risks.
- Make sure you as the facilitator are clear about the meeting's purpose so you can keep the meeting energy high and not get bogged down in the details.
- With a clear meeting purpose, you should be able to keep the meeting moving—and relatively short. The shorter and more productive your meeting, the more likely your co-workers will be to help you brainstorm in the future.
- Finally, as the facilitator, don't be afraid to be foolish or self-deprecating. It gives the other group members permission to be the same way. Remember what Steve Cony said, "There is no faster way of building trust and intimacy with another person (or group) than by your willingness to poke a little fun at yourself."

■ *Section Six* ■

Brainstormer's Bootcamp: How to Facilitate Creative Sessions

■ 29 ━━━━━━━━━━━━━━━

Plugging Into
Group Juice

In business days of old, a manager's department was his castle. And as the lord of his castle, the manager would lower his drawbridge to the outside world (other company departments, or the customer) only when he deemed it safe or necessary to do so. The lord manager spent much of his time protecting his fiefdom lest his power be usurped by other, more ruthless lord managers. The system made for great political intrigue, but frustrated the hell out of outsiders in need of supplies or services. Who, after all, wants to wait three weeks for a lousy wheel for his cart, hay for her ox, or a new blade for the plow simply because the lord manager can't get his act together? It's easier now just to move on to friendlier kingdoms.

Global competition has forced American business to reorganize from its traditional hierarchical structure of management (and the attendant fortress mentality) to a cross-functional, interdepartmental, interdependent style of doing business. Serving the king is still what it's all about. But where once management/the boss was king, now truly the customer is king.

As businesses shift to interdepartmental and interdependent ways of doing business in order to increase their own efficiency while at the same time attempting to provide better service to the customer, it is no surprise that "cross-functional teams" have become so critical to their revitalization. The scope of business problem solving has made a fundamental shift, from solving problems *within* departments to solving problems *between* departments.

The ability, then, to design, facilitate, and indeed optimize the benefits of cross-functional team meetings will play an increasingly important role in both the careers of successful managers and the level of success a company ultimately will enjoy in the marketplace.

Problem solving (and ideally *creative* problem solving) is, and will continue to be, the most important raison d'être of a well-managed cross-functional team. If you find yourself assigned to lead such a team, I hope you'll find value in some of the following recommendations.

A Brainstormer's Nightmare

I begin with an anecdote from one of my brainstorming nightmares to illustrate several important principles of the creative group process.

A good friend, Dick Mathews, president of the Stamford, Connecticut, consulting firm Mathews and Company, had called me in to do some facilitation work for one of his clients, a leading defense contractor. Dick specializes in doing internal customer satisfaction surveys, and he had just completed an extensive survey on behalf of the client. The survey revealed a number of service shortcomings in one of the company's data processing divisions and so it seemed like a good idea (at least at the time) to bring me in to conduct a creative problem-solving session on "how to improve customer service."

Twenty of the division's top managers and service administrators were assembled, I was introduced, and there we were ready to brainstorm some new ideas. Or so I thought.

The first hour of our meeting had been devoted to reviewing the survey results as a way of helping us all identify the problem areas that needed the brainstorming work. But since the results, at least in some areas, were not particularly good, it soon became apparent that many of the managers were both angry and defensive. Not a particularly healthy environment for generating new ideas, now is it?

■ ■ ■

As the anger grew, I knew it was going to be, at best, a long day. The question was, what should I, or could I, do to make the day productive? I did know that before we could hope to accomplish anything at all, we'd need to get the anger out. Otherwise, we'd just be kidding ourselves.

So I did something I very seldom do in a brainstorming session. I intentionally asked a question that I knew would trigger a judgmental, angry, and negative response.

"By the way, what areas from the survey do you want to brainstorm?" I asked somewhat innocently.

The response was both immediate and powerful. You might say the dam burst. Everyone angrily insisted that the survey results weren't valid, or it was mostly top management's fault (lack of support), or they had inherited bad systems anyway, or blah, blah, blah, blah, blah! I asked a few nonjudgmental, prompting questions as the session proceeded (what do you mean by that? is that true of all groups? does everyone agree on this?) but for the most part I stayed out of it.

Intuitively, I knew that to be an effective leader of the brainstorming session, I had to distance myself from the anger-release part of the session. I couldn't become identified with the past failures and still be an effective catalyst for new ideas. As it was, I had come in with the "survey guy," so already I was part of the enemy camp.

And so I continued to hang back. I knew that Dick Mathews was wondering why, as the facilitator, I wasn't doing my job. So much for my supposed ability to lead effective, nonjudgmental brainstorming sessions. This was turning into a hostile free-for-all; some might say it was getting ugly.

And still I hung back.

I began to feel the frustration in the room build to a level that I can only describe as "frantic tenseness." By God, someone had to take charge—and, not surprisingly, someone did.

One of the senior managers literally got up out of his seat and started directing. He called on people, pleaded, cajoled; at times he even became quite dictatorial. But at least now that terrible indecision was gone. The group had a leader.

It wasn't long before I sensed my chance to take back control of the group. The anger was gone, everyone had had his or her say, and we were ready to do some true brainstorming work. Since I was still in the front of the room, marker pen in hand, with flip charts at the ready, it was relatively easy for me to get back my leadership role by simply starting to write ideas down and asking "tell me more"-type questions. As it turned out, the senior manager and I, for all intents and purposes, ended up co-facilitating the group. He became the disciplinarian "bad cop"; I was the ever-open, sensitive, nonjudgmental "good cop." Incredible as it may seem, we really did get some terrific ideas out of that session.

Leading a Brainstorming Session

Just as nature abhors a vacuum, a group abhors a leaderless meeting. So, recommendation 1: Unless you've got a very good reason not to (as I think I did in this case), if you've been asked to lead a group, then lead it. Just as every child needs a parent, every group needs a leader. Take charge. Assign. Dictate (without being dictatorial). Cajole. Charm. Listen. Laugh. Ask question after question after question. Have fun. A group wants and needs to be led. If you as the leader don't, someone else will have to.

What does it take to successfully lead a group? Three things. One is energy and enthusiasm. Leading a group, much like performing on stage or giving a motivational speech, requires that you "outflow energy" to help build the group's spirit and enthusiasm. Think of yourself as a kind of human electrical outlet filled with juice just waiting to flow through you. If you're not letting the group members plug into your power source, believe me, there are not going to be many light bulbs flashing on in your session. The mental wattage just won't be there.

Second, try to take, and keep, the attention off yourself. This will come with practice. Ideally, when you're leading well, you will be both empty (with few or no preconceived ideas) and "in the moment." Much like a Zen master, if you can attain this state of "empty nowness," you'll be the perfect vessel for facilitating the ideas and insights of each group member. You'll be listening intently to what everyone has to say, and ultimately helping the group get the most creative mileage out of each contributed idea.

Third (and somewhat of a contradiction to point 2), you need to pay attention to your feelings. All the creative techniques in the world won't get you anywhere if you're not being sensitive to what your gut is telling you. If you're feeling uneasy about where the group is (or isn't) going, there's a reason for it. Don't be afraid to explore these feelings with the group. Paradoxically, you may find, as I often have, that if you can learn not to be afraid of what's not working, you'll get back to work a lot faster. It takes sensitivity to read the emotional climate of the group, and courage to explore with the group what may *not* be being said. If you can be honest about your feelings, the group will be honest with you about theirs. If you want a rule of thumb, it's this: What you're most afraid of doing is exactly what you should be doing.

■ 30

Where's the Fun?

"Do you think we should call the fire marshall?"

"Nah. It should burn off in a few seconds. It'll smell a little funny, but then it should be okay."

What eventually burned away was the Silly String on the chandelier overhead. (You remember Silly String: It was the stuff Tom Hanks shot from his nose in the movie *Big*.) Our brainstorming session had gotten a tad out of hand, and someone had managed to cover me (the facilitator) with the stuff, and a good part of the room as well. We all looked a little sheepish, like junior high kids who had been caught shooting spitballs, when the steward came in to bring us more refreshments for the afternoon session.

"Could he smell the stuff burning?" I wondered. No, he didn't even seem to notice. We had gotten away with it.

And then it suddenly dawned on me, we weren't kids to be reprimanded. We were the customer! We were the ones paying this hotel some ridiculously exorbitant fee to use its conference room for a day. The steward's job wasn't to scold us kids. It was to wait on us adults.

This was several years ago. I had taken a major risk in the design of a new product brainstorming session for a leading food company. I took the risk because I knew most of the session participants would be relatively young—in their late twenties and early thirties. And as with all "good" risks, I felt relatively confident that it would work. The downside was that if it didn't work, I would appear foolish and entirely unprofessional.

I knew, both from my own facilitating experience and from the research, that the best and most productive creative sessions were, above all, fun: Fun for the facilitator to facilitate and fun for the participants to be a part of. So the obvious question was, How could I make creative sessions more fun? The answer, at least to me, was also obvious: Bring in toys and games to the session, and let people "play."

Lincoln logs, yo-yos, hula hoops, dart guns, Pez, Silly Putty, Nerf Balls, superballs, Silly String: I was a kid in a candy shop/toy store. Four hundred fifty dollars later I was ready to begin my experiment. I packed two large duffel bags with the toys and boarded a plane for a Midwest conference center. There was no turning back now.

I knew from the second the clients walked into the room that I had won my gamble. One only had to look at the expressions on their faces.

There was wonder and delight, and playful expectation. I can't say that it felt quite like Disney World, but it was close. There's nothing quite like a room full of toys for setting the right mood for a creative session. Toys as creative props have since become a staple of most of my creative sessions, especially when we're working on a new product development assignment.

Playing at Creativity

Does all this sound like a little much? A little too childish? Or maybe even a case of just trying too hard? Before you scoff at the idea, consider that there are some very sound psychological principles at work behind the design of these playful creative sessions. For one, it's a way to let your participants know, right off the bat, that this creative session is going to be a fun, hopefully nonthreatening event. Many people, especially first timers, come to a creative session scared to death. Part of the reason is simply not knowing what to expect, having a natural fear of the unknown. But there is also the fear of not being creative, especially when there's the added pressure of having to be creative in a group. Anything the facilitator can do to alleviate some of this fear is a good thing.

Consider also that when people are in a relaxed, playful, and fun-loving state, they are more likely to *make unexpected creative connections.* Their minds are free from judgment and worry, and therefore free to free-associate. If you doubt this, try coming up with a new idea when you're afraid or angry. It's very hard, if not impossible, to do.

Also toys and games, from a psychological/neurological-conditioning standpoint, are linked in most adults' memories with the play and fun of childhood. What quicker way, then, to elicit the childhood state than to use the toys we all played with as children as psychological memory triggers?

There's also the possibility (more likely than you might think) that one or more of these toys might help to stimulate an exciting new product idea.

Finally, the toys make the session breaks more fun. Invariably, someone will pick up a Nerf football or tennis ball and start passing it back and forth. This helps build team spirit in the group, as well as providing a welcome physical release from the mentally taxing process of brainstorming.

This brings me to three anecdotes on the value of play in the creative process. These stories are about as different as you can get, except that all three do point to the value of having fun in the creative process. I call these anecdotes the paper clip bullet, the wet-tongued napkin, and looking for mister longstocking, respectively.

The Paper Clip Bullet

During World War II, my late father, J. Clarke "Matti" Mattimore, was part of a special propaganda unit made up of some of the nation's most talented idea men: advertising executives, Pulitzer-prize winning authors, and award-winning photographers and graphic designers. I remember two things in particular that he told me about being in this unit: First, he said, it was the happiest and most fulfilling time of his life, and second, it was like going to an out-of-control kindergarten classroom every day. These guys were constantly horsing around and getting in all kinds of trouble—paper airplanes out the window, shooting paper clip "bullets" at their commanding officer, all kinds of entirely juvenile pranks. They also did some of the finest creative work—recruitment posters in particular—of any single creative group in the war. I always felt that their brilliant creative work and their continual horsing around must somehow be related. I now know that they were. True creativity is, as one philosopher put it, an act of destruction, exchanging the old for the new, the tried for the never been tried, the conventional for the original. To be creative, you must be dissatisfied with the status quo. You must challenge authority. This horsing around was challenging the status quo. The group's creative work also was challenging the status quo.

By the way, if you are wondering how they were able to get away with their creative tomfoolery, it was because they were all officers. Apparently, short of a court-martial, it is very difficult to take disciplinary action against an officer. They knew that despite his threats, the commanding officer was not going to court-martial them for shooting paper clips. Imagine how foolish he'd look filing the charges.

The Wet-Tongued Napkin

I'm always interested in what thoughts lead to a breakthrough idea. For an article I was researching on play and the creative process, I came across a team of inventors in Chicago that had an interesting story to tell. Henry Arias and Denise Heimrich founded their Chicago-based company Thinking Heads several years ago to invent and license new toys and games. They went out to lunch one day, and in a playful mood, Denise, as a child might, picked up a napkin and stuck her wet tongue through it at her partner. She started laughing, but her partner Henry suggested, "We might have something here." For some time they had been trying to invent a very low cost, simple action game for young kids. Until Denise put her tongue through the napkin, they had been coming up somewhat dry. The tongue through the napkin bit of childlike spontaneity was the creative spark that inspired Denise and Henry to invent the successful game Thin Ice. If you haven't seen Thin Ice, it is ingeniously simple. Kids spread a tissue over a raised platform to form the "ice." Below the "ice" is a water-filled reservoir with marbles in it. Kids pick up the wet marbles with "ice tongs" and place them, one by one, on the tissue. The first kid to add the marble that "breaks through the thin ice" (like Denise's wet tongue going through the napkin) loses. Simple, fun—and very inexpensive to produce.

Looking for Mister Longstocking

Finally, in a somewhat less frivolous, but no less playful invention, I have a story about the commercialization of nylon. Many people know that DuPont research chemist Dr. Wallace Carothers invented nylon (known then as Polymer 66) in 1934. What many people do not know is that virtually nothing was done with the invention (it wasn't even patented) until Julian Hill, a colleague of Carothers', found a way to increase the tensile strength of Carothers' basic discovery. One day, while playing around with the substance, Hill noticed that he could stretch the strands of the material quite far into a thin string. In a bit of creative horseplay, apparently when Carothers, the lab director, had gone downtown to run an errand, Hill got together a number of his co-workers to run down the halls of the office building to see how far they could stretch the stuff. As it stretched further and further down the hallway, they noticed that the extended strands were becoming quite silky in appearance. This silkiness signaled to the engineers that the molecules of the polymer were lining up, and that the strength of the substance would therefore increase, which was exactly what had happened. Hill's discovery became known as the cold-drawing process and led to the commercialization of nylon, DuPont's most important and successful product ever.[1]

So, what's the moral of these anecdotes? It's this: When it comes to creativity, if you haven't learned how to play, you haven't learned how to work.

Note

1. Royston M. Roberts, *Serendipity* (New York: John Wiley & Sons, 1989), p. 173.

═ *31* ═

Tricks of the Idea Trade: Let's Risk It!

There are two inviolable rules of brainstorming. One is, separate the idea generation stage of the process from the judgmental stage; the other is, generate as many ideas as you can because ultimately quantity breeds quality. But of course, all rules, especially when it comes to creativity and the creative process, are made to be broken. These two are certainly no exceptions.

That being said, I thought I'd share some of the brainstorming tricks of the trade I have learned over the years. By no means are they rules, and even if they were, my advice to you would be to break them—and often.

In and Out Thinking

Research has shown that if John Muschutto, the former fast-talking Federal Express "spokesperson," were able to talk almost twice as fast as his fastest, we could still understand him. Most of us talk at about 120 words per minute. Network news commentators speak at the rate of about 160 words per minute. Muschutto clocks in at 365 words per minute. But research with the visually impaired shows that with some practice, we can still understand what's going on at 600 words per minute or more. Quite incredible, isn't it?

The implication for the brainstorming facilitator, and for the seminar participant, is that no matter how fast or compelling the things that one may be saying are, each of us has three to four times as much "in-between" time to think about other things. In the psychological literature, this is known as in and out thinking. The "in" time is when you're concentrating on what the speaker is saying. The "out" time is when you're thinking about other, often unrelated things: what you had for breakfast, what to get your wife or husband for a birthday, when you're going to paint the house. If you like, think of the out time as daydreaming.

Research has also shown, not surprisingly, that out time increases when the listener perceives the subject matter being presented as boring or uninteresting. Paradoxically, the more a presenter (or a teacher) tries to force the listener to stay in (Johnny! Are you listening to me?), the more likely the listener is to go out.

In any brainstorming session (especially in an all-day affair), obviously you are going to have a great deal of in and out thinking going on. The trick for the facilitator is not to prevent out thinking (which is impossible anyway), but to acknowledge it as a natural part of the process and give the participants the freedom they need, both physically and mentally, to help them get back in when they realize they are spending more time out than in.

Allowing people to do physical things and not be tied down to a chair all day is the most effective way I know of to help people get back in. By allowing and indeed encouraging physical distractions, mental out time and daydreaming will be significantly reduced. Therefore, as the facilitator, you should encourage your participants to stand up when they feel like standing, doodle when they feel like doodling, and play with a toy when they feel like playing.

I remember once facilitating a half-day session for a group of high-energy salespeople. This was an extraordinary group of mostly men: smart, personable, and honest. They also had an extremely high level of energy, both as a group and individually. I knew it would be a challenge to keep them motivated and "in" the process.

Encouraging them to get up and walk around gave their physical energy an outlet, so that they could more efficiently focus their mental energy on the task at hand. The result was that we had a very productive session together. It was wonderful to see their energy and enthusiasm being so powerfully brought to bear on the problem. Do you know that when we finally arrived at our breakthrough idea (a new selling strategy), almost everyone was literally standing around me in a kind of makeshift football huddle? It was as if we had somehow just won the big game together. It was tremendously exciting.

It makes you wonder, doesn't it, why we force our kids to sit at desks at school all day?

What's the Risk?

If you've read other books on creativity in business, you're probably familiar with the name George Prince. For many years, George was the president of Synetics, the Cambridge, Massachusetts, consulting firm that literally invented creativity consulting in the early 1960s. The first time I met George, I was taking the Synetics "Connections" course in an effort to improve my creative facilitating skills. My first, very distinct impression of George was that he was what I can only call a master of openness. My sense of the man was that like some kind of egoless Zen master, he had developed within himself a true nonjudgmental openness to new ideas and experiences.

In a subsequent half-day meeting with George, I had the opportunity to exchange creative war stories and learn some of what he had learned about group creativity in the last thirty years. In essence, he said that the key to successful group process could be summarized in a single word: risk. The primary job of the facilitator is to establish a climate where each participant can feel safe taking risks. Like all timeless truths, it's simple, but not necessarily easy.

I remember my first formal brainstorming session at a large New York ad agency shortly after graduating from college. I walked into that session as an open, trusting, somewhat naive "idea kid" who was looking to contribute as many ideas as he could to "land that new airline account." I walked out totally disillusioned, and kind of sad. It was a shock to see the president of the agency, someone I had previously respected, throw a kind of psychic power net over the entire proceedings. That supposed brainstorming session wasn't about creating new ideas. It was about politics and power and fear and manipulation.

Building Trust

This brings up an interesting point about the makeup of a brainstorming group. In my experience, the single most important question you as facilitator can ask is, Who will be the most senior member or boss in the group, and what is his or her relationship with the other participants? Unless you have a truly superior manager, someone who really does believe in empowering the people that work for him or her, you may be in for a less than stellar session. If the relationship between "the boss" and his or her co-workers is about power, and therefore fear, you're not going to be seeing a great deal of creative risk taking among the other members of the group. And without risk taking, you have little hope of getting a truly original idea.

A case in point is a series of three creativity training and brainstorming sessions I ran for the Los Angeles manufacturing plant of an international packaged goods marketer. In all three sessions we had a wide range of ethnically diverse participants from all levels and departments within the company, along with a senior manager. Sessions one and three were two of the best sessions I've ever conducted. We generated some great ideas, and without exception the group participants greatly appreciated the creativity training. Credit for the success of these sessions was due, in no small part, to the genuine desire of the two senior managers to empower their employees.

And then there was session two. Ratings in this session were the lowest we had ever gotten, averaging below five on a ten-point scale (the two other sessions averaged 9.4). What could account for such widely divergent ratings when all three sessions had the same basic design and facilitator?

Feelings of fear, rather than a desire to empower, were the difference. Session two had an insecure and, in my opinion, bitter and unhappy boss in charge. Some of his power plays were subtle; others were blatantly aggressive attacks. Those brave souls who did speak up were quickly beaten down, despite my attempts to defend them, and the others in the group quickly learned that the safest thing to do was to just keep quiet. The irony was that by the end of the day, after relentless attempts on my part to build some level of trust and creative risk taking, the guy finally did start to come around. When we got past his insecurities (masked by an aura of presumed self-confidence), he actually proved to be quite talented and creative. Even some members of the group began to catch the spirit and make valuable contributions. It was a shame, though, that we had to waste most of the day dealing with this guy's insecurities before we could make any progress.

By the way, if you're interested in how one goes about trying to build some level of trust in this kind of situation, my approach has always been to enlist the problem person as a kind of ally. Recognizing that a problem person's fears and insecurities often translates to a need to be in control, I ask them for advice on how to proceed with the facilitating of the session, "since this is obviously a more difficult assignment than we had previously thought." With this tack, all but the most cynical of bosses will quickly become the facilitator's ally and make all kinds of suggestions, often surprisingly good ones, as to how best to proceed.

32

Sex and Other Tricks of the Idea Trade

Sex, sex, sex. Concerns about the issue of sexual harassment aside, one surefire way to know that your brainstorming session is "happening" is when you, the facilitator, begin to hear the participants throw out quips, jests, japes, and jokes that are rife with sexual innuendo. When this happens, invariably you know you're well on your way to having a good session.

However, don't expect the sexual knee- (or would that be thigh?) slappers to start right away. It takes some building before the sexual innuendoes, or, if you're lucky, blatantly sexual remarks, occur. Generally, the group starts out with some good-natured joking: nothing particularly risqué, just some polite witticisms. This is stage one in the loosening-up process. The best session participants will invariably have a good sense of humor anyway (often mixed with a liberal dose of irreverence), so it's not surprising that pretty quickly, even during the introductions, someone will start making wisecracks.

Then, as the group members get to know each other better and feel more comfortable with one another, the jokes become increasingly off-color and risqué. All in all, it's a very natural process, this progression from polite, witty banter to total debauchery. It's an evolution, though, that can't and shouldn't be forced by the facilitator. The goal of total debauchery much like the feeling among best friends, has to evolve over time and emerge naturally out of the collective group consciousness. Some groups never reach it. Other groups, especially if they're filled with "characters" (wild and crazy creative types), almost always do.

Why is sexual innuendo an important barometer of the evolution of a group? It's a signal that the formal has yielded to the informal, that repression has given way to spontaneity, that fear has been replaced by fun, and ultimately that posturing has been superseded by honesty. In my experience, there is also no better demonstration that a feeling of mutual trust has been built among the group members than having jokes about sex. Think about it. Would you tell a dirty joke to someone you didn't know well? Of course you wouldn't. If you did, most likely you'd be perceived as a pervert, especially if you were talking to a member of the opposite sex. It's only really good friends with whom we feel comfortable being perverted.

Without getting overly Freudian about it, I think you'll agree that we're fairly repressed sexually in this country. So when a group of strangers, or even co-workers for that matter, can get together and feel comfortable enough with one another to bring up, even indirectly through joking, our most taboo and repressed subject of all, sex, then you know you're on to something. Guards have been let down sufficiently for the participants to actually say the first thing that comes to their minds, without feeling afraid that they'll be made to look foolish or, worse yet, perverted. And when you get this kind of spontaneity, you can't help but get true creativity as well.

I can remember one creativity training session I did for a group of high-tech salespeople. Without in any way trying to disparage the fundamentalist religious point of view, I've got to tell you that this one fellow, who was the devoutest of devout fundamentalists, was the most difficult "student" I have ever had. He could not, in any way, allow himself to even entertain the possibility that the training session could be of some value to him, much less fun. He was there only because his boss had told him he had to be.

Closed-minded as he was, I also had to admire the guy. True to his belief, when we did the final debriefing on what he had learned from the day's training, he said, "absolutely nothing—it was a complete and total waste of my time." Yes, I had to admit, I did respect the guy's honesty, and indeed courage, in expressing his unique point of view. Honesty is an important personality characteristic of the best brainstorming participants. Honest as this guy was, though, somehow he'd not have been my first choice to head a team of all-star brainstormers. His fundamentalist point of view didn't seem to include the word "fun"—or much of a sense of humor, for that matter, which is also a personality trait of the best brainstormers.

To Post or Not to Post?

Most facilitators use the rather archaic system of recording ideas on flip chart paper and then posting these sheets around the room as they fill up with ideas. Of course, there are now electronic blackboards on the market that will give you an 8 1/2 by 11 printout of anything you've written on a large blackboard. Unfortunately, because of the limited electronic blackboard space, you won't have a running record of your ideas that you can post around the room. (Yes, you could post the 8 1/2 by 11 printouts, but obviously these would be too small to be of much practical value to the group.)

This is a case where I think the older way is the better way. By posting the flip chart sheets with often hundreds of ideas on them, you have a concrete record of the group's progress for everyone to see. Also, you can't help but build a sense of achievement in the group as the room literally fills up with ideas. Psychologically, this is a very positive and powerful thing to do.

There is also a more pragmatic reason to post ideas. When the ideas are displayed around the room, they will often trigger even more new ideas. Sometimes, for instance, a participant will see an idea and have a "build" on that idea that suddenly makes it viable, or potentially more exciting. Other times a posted idea will trigger an entirely new concept. Occasionally, someone will make a connection between two seemingly unrelated ideas that makes for an even more exciting third idea. In fact, it's often a good exercise at the end of the day to have everyone walk around the room looking for ways to combine "old" ideas into "new" ideas.

I remember, for instance, a session I did for the Connecticut Urban League (a nonprofit inner-city job training organization) to generate new fund-raising programs. At one end of the room was an idea to start an executive networking service so that current corporate contributors could help us recruit new corporate contributors. At the other end of the room was an idea to find out the favorite causes (literacy training, AIDS, employment, housing for the homeless, etc.) of the most powerful local CEOs and see if the Urban League might help in some way to further those causes, in return for a donation. It was natural to combine the two ideas to make each more practical, focused, and doable. The concept: Use the executive network to do the research for us. It gave the executive networkers an excuse to call other CEOs other than just for fund-raising and it promised them a warmer reception when they actually did call because they were asking about the CEO's favorite cause.

Finally, posting the ideas around the room makes it easier to bring the group to closure and have group members pick the ideas that they think are the most exciting and have the greatest potential for further development.

Dot Voting

As you may know, a critical element of any brainstorming session is withholding judgment. Any and all ideas, no matter how outrageous, should be given the space to grow or evolve into workable ideas. How, then, do you maintain this feeling of nonjudgmental acceptance that the group has built up over the course of a session when it comes time to be a hard-nosed realist and begin selecting the best ideas for further development? Essentially, you're looking for a way to be nonjudgmentally judgmental. I use a technique I call "dot voting."

To dot vote, all you need are a few sheets of different-colored Avery Label stick-on dots (available at your local office supply store). Each brainstormer, with dots in hand, simply walks around the room and "votes" for each "best idea" by sticking a dot next to it. In ten minutes (or less) it becomes obvious which ideas the group considers to be the winners. It's a fast, fun, entirely democratic, and, most important, non-judgmental way to "judge" the group's best ideas.

■ *33* ━━━━━━━━━━━━━━━

The Facilitator as Star

It didn't take long, maybe thirty seconds, to know that these people in the session from manufacturing and production were angry, very angry. They felt, and rightly so, that they were being taken advantage of by the marketing department.

Marketing had been responsible, in large part, for the company's tremendous growth over the last five years. Marketing was the star, marketing had the power, and everyone knew it. Manufacturing had no choice but to perform for marketing, and with breakneck speed and efficiency. The future of the company depended on it.

The problem was that marketing was also scared. When you've been very successful and made some brilliant marketing decisions, sometimes the only place to go is down. Marketing began second-guessing itself and taking longer and longer to make decisions. Consequently, more and more pressure was being put on manufacturing to meet the impossible deadlines created by marketing's indecision.

One of the problems was that these manufacturing people were, in a sense, *too* good. They invariably rose to the challenge and met the impossible-to-meet deadline. And so, human nature being what it is, marketing came to take it for granted that manufacturing would and could do the impossible. Yes, manufacturing could and did. But they came to resent being taking advantage of by "the stars" (read as prima donnas) in marketing. When emergencies become commonplace, it begins to take its toll.

It was also costing the company a great deal of money in rush printing charges, wasted formulations, product overstocks, etc. The conservative estimate was that the company was spending an extra $15 million per year because of marketing's failure to make timely decisions.

We spent the first hour of our brainstorming session identifying the problem and getting the anger out. But then, with the problem well identified and the anger dissipated, the next question was, of course, what could we do to mitigate, if not solve, the problem? How could manufacturing put pressure on marketing to get them to make timely, cost-effective decisions? We began brainstorming possible solutions without much success. So I did what I often do when things aren't going well. I had the group take a break.

A break will often accomplish several useful things. For one, it helps the group members get away from the problem and encourages a level of objectivity that is difficult to achieve in the heat of a brainstorming session. Seeing the forest for the trees can be difficult, especially when you're barking up the wrong tree.

Taking a break also gives the subconscious a chance to work on the problem, even for as short a time as five or ten minutes. Somehow, magically, while you're chatting with one of your brainstorming buddies about the weather or how great the Bulls are doing, the subconscious is working away on the problem, often making unexpected associations and connections. The metaphor it brings to mind is that of a ham radio operator. When the operator's sending a message (i.e., brainstorming), he can't receive one. But when he stops sending, his radio will pick up whatever's in or on the air. For me, "what's in the air" is the same as what's waiting to be heard from the subconscious. It's like Norman Lear says, "If you let it, the subconscious will always slip you little notes with answers written on them."

Taking a break also gives the facilitator time to decide on a new direction, creativity strategy, or technique that he or she feels will have the greatest chance of success.

Occasionally, I'll even get "the answer" during the break, which was what happened in this case. This raises an interesting question about the facilitator's role in the actual generation of ideas during a session: Should the facilitator be contributing ideas?

The Facilitator as Participant?

One of the unwritten laws of brainstorming facilitating is that the facilitator should not, under any circumstances, contribute ideas. His or her job is strictly to facilitate the process, to make sure that the participants' ideas, no matter how absurd or outrageous, are respected and championed. If the facilitator is busy generating, or worse yet championing, his or her own ideas, the delicate balance between mutual trust and personal risk quickly evaporates because the facilitator's ego has gotten in the way. Obviously, he's not getting the best out of his group. Unconsciously, he's promoting a feeling of competition rather than cooperation.

Or so the conventional wisdom goes. This is one law of brainstorming with which I happen to disagree. Under certain circumstances I feel it's important and occasionally even critical, that the facilitator contribute ideas.

When is it and when is it not a good idea for the facilitator to be contributing ideas? And how can you know? The answer is, it comes down to the facilitator's intent. If the facilitator is proposing ideas for his own self-aggrandizement, then no time is the right time! As the facilitator, he's not only not helping the group realize its full potential, he's actually getting in the way of the process. If, however, the facilitator has a different motivation for throwing out ideas—namely, for them to act as catalysts to spark the group into new and different ways of thinking—then by all means this is a good thing! Sometimes, for instance, especially when I've had the large group break up into smaller brainstorming subgroups, I will move from group to group proposing what I know are absurd, ridiculous, or even comical suggestions in an effort to encourage more risk taking in the participants' thinking.

In the case of the manufacturing/marketing deadline problem, it was in discussing with my co-facilitator how to proceed with the session, that we hit upon "the answer."

■ ■ ■

"Why not," we thought, "create a new kind of timeline/PERT chart that includes not only the deadlines for marketing decisions, but also the costs associated with *not* making these decisions in time?" So, for example, in addition to the task deadline "final packaging design due by July 14," we'd also include the note: "If the packaging design decisions are not made by July 14, additional costs to the company will be approximately $10,000 for each week of delay."

This "PERT/money chart" concept has three major advantages. First, it serves as an ongoing reminder to marketing of the cost of delaying decisions. Second, it makes each executive within marketing responsible, and therefore accountable, for the cost overruns that he or his department is causing. Finally, it gives manufacturing a way of charging back to marketing the increased costs incurred by marketing's indecisiveness. All in all, not a bad idea.

So what did I do with this idea? When we came back from break, I helped the group, by leading with the right questions, to create the idea on its own.

You must understand that your goal as the facilitator is to help *the group* create exciting and original concepts. The last thing you as the facilitator want to do is try to take credit for ideas in a group session. Propose ideas, yes. Spark ideas, yes. But take credit, absolutely not! It's critical to the group energy and spirit that it be the creator of, and get credit for, *all* the ideas in the session.

■ 34

Saving the Worst
for Last

"Tell me more."
"How else could we use that?"
"Did I write down everything you were saying?"
"Does anyone have a 'build' on that idea?"
"What do you like most about his or her idea?"
"How might that work?"

If you looked at a transcript of what a skilled facilitator typically might say throughout a day-long brainstorming session, 90 percent of it wouldn't be much different from the questions and prompts you see above. These kinds of prompts serve several purposes.

First and foremost, they help participants clarify, and often further develop, very roughly formed, often sketchy ideas. Despite what any of the "experts" may tell you, brainstorming, like life, is a messy process. By its very nature, it is a random, incomplete, and ill-defined activity.

In the best sessions, participants feel free (and secure) enough to propose unfinished and ill-defined ideas based on their intuitions, mental pictures, flashes of insight, and "gut feels." Frequently, participants will say things like, "I'm not quite sure what I'm saying here," or, "I know it's kind of crazy, but there's something about that idea," or even, "This is probably a really stupid idea, but . . ." It's very important for the facilitator to be sensitive to these kind of statements and encourage them at every opportunity. Why? Because they are indications that your group members are beginning to trust one another, and that they are using right-brain, creative, and holistic modes of thinking. The right brain deals primarily in pictures and feelings, and it shouldn't surprise the facilitator that group members will often stutter and stammer to find the left-brain words to express an idea that had its origins in a right-brain feeling or mental image.

The facilitator's prompts can also help a participant develop an ill-formed, seemingly bad idea into one with great potential. The more an idea is explored and fleshed out, the more form that's added to what was previously ill-formed, the greater the potential to discover a surprising and exciting new idea. Without the facilitator's prompt, however, the idea could die before it ever has a chance at life. As with a newborn baby gasping for air, the facilitator must see to it that the idea has a chance to breathe.

There is also the possibility that as one group member is encouraged to develop his or her idea, another group member will piggyback on the original idea and either improve it or come up with a new idea altogether.

Finally, the facilitator's prompts also serve the very pragmatic purpose of giving the facilitator time to accurately record the idea on the flip chart. Often a session will have such energy, and be proceeding so quickly, that if the facilitator is not careful, participants will be calling out ideas so quickly that he or she will miss a key idea or build. The prompts can help the facilitator slow down the flow of ideas, clarify what's being said, and give the time needed to accurately record the ideas on the flip chart. Prompts help the facilitator stay in control without being controlling.

Headlining

One of the most useful of the tricks of the brainstorming trade is for the facilitator to encourage the brainstormers to phrase their ideas in the form of a headline. "Can you put your idea in a headline for me?" is the prompt.

Often such a prompt will force the participant to encapsulate seemingly endless rambling, loosely developed thoughts into a few cogent and concise words or phrases. Not only does the headline prompt help the participant distill and define his or her thinking, it makes the facilitator's job a lot easier. There is a lot less to write on the flip chart.

It also keeps the session moving and gives the facilitator a gracious way to interrupt a long-drawn-out speech (there's always one participant who feels the need to pontificate) that can adversely affect group energy and enthusiasm.

Group Energy

Facilitating will always be more of an art than a science. The best facilitators operate more by feel and intuition than by the need to adhere to a specific, predetermined schedule or plan outlining the day's creativity exercises. Above all, the facilitator needs to be sensitive to where the group wants to go. Sometimes the best thing a facilitator can do is just stay out of the way and let the group lead itself. Much like a jockey riding a prize thoroughbred, the facilitator has to let the group run when it needs to run, to loosen the reins and enjoy the ride, despite the sometimes frightening pace.

In a magical sort of way, each group has its own identity. The facilitator has the responsibility for both being a part of this group identity and directing the group's unique energies and talents into the most productive channels of creative expression.

There is a strange phenomenon that I have noticed from my years of facilitating a wide variety of groups and an eclectic assortment of creative assignments. In almost all the groups, I feel a certain sense of inevitability, or destiny if you will, of the ideas that ultimately emerge from the brainstorming session. It's as if the ideas were already there in the ether somehow, hovering just above the group, waiting for their time to be "discovered." Maybe it's because the best ideas are always simple and obvious, and invariably have that "why didn't I think of that before?" feeling to them.

At some level, though, probably deep within the individual's (or the group's) subconscious mind(s), I believe that *they really did think of that idea before*. Like Michelangelo chipping away at a block of stone to "reveal the work of art already inside," I've come to see the facilitator's role as one of simply helping to reveal the ideas that have *already been created*.

Of course, occasionally you run into a group that you couldn't cut through with a sledge hammer (much less Michelangelo's hammer and chisel), but that's a different story. Deep down, way down, there's an idea waiting to get out; it just may not happen in our lifetime.

A final word of advice to the would-be facilitator or group leader: Do not try to artificially manipulate a group's creative flow, either through mock cheerleading when things are not going well or by imposing a creative technique when the group is doing fine without one. You'll only tire yourself— and the group—out. Recognize that there are peaks and valleys in any creativity session. Sometimes the energy level will be high and the group excited; other times it will be low and the group seemingly out of gas. This is natural and to be expected. To get over the low-energy times, take more frequent breaks. Or have the group do something physical like jumping jacks or ceiling stretches for five or ten minutes. Or consider changing your physical environment (a good time is usually 2:30 or 3:00 in the afternoon, when the group's energy is traditionally at its lowest point), and go for an "idea walk."

Saving the Worst for Last

I wanted to give you one last brainstormer's trick of the trade. This is an (almost) never-fail technique for breaking creative log jams, and coming up with a breakthrough idea. It's also a lot of fun.

It's called "the worst idea," and as its name implies, everyone in this exercise tries to come up with a really bad idea—in fact, the worst possible idea he or she can possibly think of. (To add a little creative and competitive excitement to this exercise, consider giving a prize for the all-time *worst* idea.) Stupid as this technique sounds, you'd be amazed how powerful a creative exercise it can be and how difficult it often is to think of a really bad idea. Invariably, someone will propose what initially, truth be told, does sound like a bad idea (often it's quite funny) but then, human nature (and the competitive spirit) being what it is, someone else will find a way to turn this really bad idea into something quite good, and occasionally brilliant.

I think there are three reasons why this technique will work when all others fail. For one, it takes away all the performance pressure "to get that really great idea." People relax and say whatever comes to mind.

Second, it's fun and funny, which, of course, is an essential ingredient in any successful session.

And finally, it employs the principle of opposites. As with yin and yang, hills and valleys, cold and warm, light and shadow, you can't have one without the other. So by looking for the worst idea, you often can't help but see the best idea, too. Take the campaign for the California raisins. When copywriters Seth Werner and Dextor Fedor were trying to brainstorm a campaign to promote California raisins, they were getting nowhere. Until, that is, they went over to a friend's house to work, and Werner happened to mockingly propose having the raisins "do something stupid like singing, 'Heard it through the Grapevine.' Everyone laughed and forgot about what was obviously a ridiculous idea until the next morning, when, upon reflection, absurd as it was, the idea seemed to have some merit. It wasn't long before Werner and partner Fedor had contacted Claymation creator Will Vinton, and one of advertising's most memorable and effective campaigns was born.

Index